The Mark Spitz
Complete Book of Swimming

The Mark Spitz Complete Book of Swimming

Mark Spitz and Alan LeMond

Photographs by Neil Leifer

Thomas Y. Crowell Company
Established 1834   New York

Manufactured in the United States of America

Library of Congress Cataloging in Publication Data

Spitz, Mark.
    The Mark Spitz complete book of swimming.

    Includes index.
    1. Swimming.   I. LeMond, Alan, joint author.
II. Leifer, Neil.   III. Title.
GV837.S815   797.2'1   73-42490
ISBN 0-690-00690-X

10 9 8 7 6 5 4 3 2 1

Contents

The Mark Spitz
Complete Book of Swimming

Introduction

A SUPERSTAR during the 1972 Olympics and for some time thereafter, Mark Spitz won an unprecedented seven gold medals, accompanied by universal acclaim for his monumental feat. He also earned a place in pop history when he became the second best-selling pinup ever—second only to Betty Grable. The tremendous adulation he received from an adoring public reached a peak during the year that followed his victories and gradually subsided until what was left was a worldwide respect for the athletic achievement he had demonstrated—a respect that was granite solid, for the Olympic records he set will endure for a long, long time to come and may never be broken.

How did he achieve such remarkable swimming records? What qualities made him one of the all-time great swimmers—if not *the* greatest swimmer ever? It certainly wasn't magic. It was a great deal of disciplined and dedicated hard work.

In this book Mark Spitz describes what he feels enabled him to achieve his spectacular Olympic feats: his interpretation of the correct way to swim. This book is designed to help you relax and feel more comfortable in the water, and to enable you to take pleasure in the exhilarating sport of swimming. But, if you are so inclined, it will also help you to begin your training for future athletic—and possibly Olympic—success.

Mark Spitz is an excellent example of a person who combined natural ability with a strong, dedicated will to succeed. And he did succeed—admirably. He has already accomplished a great deal, more than most of us will accomplish in a lifetime, and he is still only in his twenties. It will not be surprising when he accomplishes much more, for the discipline and training that were so important for his successful Olympic quest are certainly no hindrance to whatever else he may wish to pursue. And in such pursuit the demonstrated fact that he is no quitter makes every task he pursues, with concentrated effort, a sure bet. We may well look forward to yet another Spitz spectacular in whatever new field he may choose.

Married to the very attractive and personable Susan Weiner Spitz, a model and actress, Mark is already "testing the water" in such diverse areas as skiing, sailing, acting, and some commercial business ventures . . . where there are records yet to be set. Of his past records, this summary of what he has earned says it best:

> 32 world records, 25 in individual events and 7 in relays, 1967–1972; 9 gold, 1 silver, and 1 bronze medal in the Olympic Games, 1968 and 1972; 5 gold medals, Pan American Games, 1967; first place 8 times, second place once, and third place twice in NCAA championships, 1969–1972; first place 24 times, second place 6 times, and third place once in AAU championships, 1966–1972; Sullivan Award, 1971; AAU Swimming Award, 1972; World Swimmer of the Year, 1967, 1971, and 1972.

Mark, who had been breaking swimming records from his earliest competitions, broke seven more during the 1972 Olympics in Munich (Olympiad XX) and achieved worldwide fame. Here was an athlete who was in as complete command of his sport as any other athlete in Olympic history. He dominated the 1972 Olympics, right up through the ceremony that awarded him his seventh medal. The entire world was caught up in his golden quest and avidly followed his progress as he racked up victory after victory. In the first event he entered—the 200-meter butterfly, he knocked off .83 seconds from his own world record of 2m.01.53 to win the first of his seven gold medals.

In the next event, the 400-meter freestyle relay, he helped his teammates heat up the pool for another record and another medal. The third followed in the 200-meter freestyle, the fourth in the 100-meter butterfly, the fifth in the 800-meter freestyle relay, and the sixth and seventh were won—respectively—in the 100-meter freestyle and the 400-meter medley relay. It was a record-breaking event. Never before in the history of modern Olympics had one person achieved so much.

Mark Spitz says that he accomplished it all simply by swimming faster than anyone else, but his twelve years of strenuous, constant training might have had something to do with it, as could his impressive physical characteristics. Certainly these factors couldn't have hurt him any—in or out of the pool.

He carries his well-developed body easily and confidently, demonstrating the finely toned muscles that years of swimming have given him. His hands are large and scoop-shaped and his chest gives every indication of being broad enough to carry sufficient oxygen to supply his needs no matter how long the race. Both are physical attributes that would give him a nice boost up to the top of the swimming ladder in themselves, but he also has the unusual ability of being able to flex his knees forward in such a manner as to give himself a thrust that goes six to twelve inches deeper in the water than that of his competitors.

Sherman Chavoor, his coach for many years, once said of Spitz that he is "so loose and long muscled (that) the way he slips through the water is thoroughly mystifying."

It was acknowledged early in his career, by those who knew swimming and swimmers, that Mark Spitz might well become the best swimmer in the world one day. Even before he enrolled in college, he had a good start toward fulfilling that prophesy. At that point he had broken ten swimming records.

The fantastic record-breaking career of Mark Andrew Spitz is a long story, but in brief and in Mark's words, it goes this way:

"The first record I ever set was an age group record in the butterfly stroke. I was ten years old and I tied with a buddy of mine. I think the time was 31 seconds flat in the 50-yard butterfly in a 25-yard pool.

"I was trained as a distance swimmer when I was young, and that enabled me at a later date to be a sprinter since I had been conditioned for the long haul—for endurance. In sprints, it's the swimmer who can hold out the longest—at a high rate of speed—who wins. And it is much easier, I feel, to go from distance to sprints than it is to go from sprints to distance.

"My training was constant. It would start in the summer, just swimming, maybe going 2,000 yards, then continually building up so that by the end of September I would enter a schedule that was pretty substantial. At that point I was doing about 10,000 yards in one workout, which took between two and two and a half hours. That would continue until the indoor nationals in March or April.

"Then I would take a week or two off before starting the long course training. This took place in a 50-meter pool, training two hours a day until I got out of college for the summer. Then I'd go home to California and train. In the summer I'd train about two and a half hours in the morning and an hour to an hour and forty-five minutes in the afternoon. And I did that up until the outdoor nationals.

"The first time I ever won a national championship I was sixteen years old in Lincoln, Nebraska. I won the 100-meter butterfly and my time was 58.2 seconds. The world record, I think, at that time was 57 seconds flat. I broke the record the next year when I was seventeen with a time of 56.3 seconds.

"Five years later in the 1972 Olympics, I set a new world's record of 2.00.7 in the 200-meter butterfly. I was swimming twice as far and going almost as fast as when I set the earlier butterfly records.

"I concentrated on what I was doing during my swimming career and made few mistakes, such as swimming the wrong stroke in a race—a butterfly stroke in a breaststroke event, for instance. But once I did make a mistake, which was quite funny at the time. I swam too many laps.

"It was a 500-yard freestyle event and I was about sixteen or seventeen years old. My competitors and I were supposed to swim 20 laps in a 25-yard pool. I was going for a record and I put on the sprint for the last two laps. There was only one problem. I had already finished the race before I started sprinting.

"My time for the race was something like a half a second off the record, which meant I would have broken the record if I had put the push on when I should have. But I still felt good about it, because even though I did swim two extra laps, I came in first.

"In my whole career, I broke thirty-five swimming records of which ten were broken in my last year of swimming. Of course, breaking records works this way. Assume that a record for some event is 60 seconds flat and I swim the event in 59.8. The next time out I swim it in 59.6, and the next time in 59.1. It would be recognized that chronologically I broke the record three times, even if I was breaking my own record twice.

"My first coach, when I was ten, was Sherman Chavoor. He coached the Arden Hills Swim and Tennis Club and then because my father's work took him to Oakland, I swam for a couple of years with the Aqua Bears in Oakland, California, coached by a woman named Laurabelle Brooksaver. Then I joined the Pleasant Hill Swim Club where I was coached by Irvin Zader. I swam with the Aqua Bears and the Pleasant Hill Swim Club when I was between the ages of twelve and fourteen. Then I went to high school at Santa Clara and swam for George Haines between the ages of fourteen and eighteen.

"At eighteen I attended Indiana University where I was coached for four years by James (Doc) Counsilman during the college season. In the summers I went back to Sherman Chavoor in Sacramento where my parents lived at the time.

"Sherman Chavoor was also the coach who worked with me for the Olympics. The Olympic coach chosen by the Olympic Committee was Peter Daland, but that position is more honorary than anything else. Sherman Chavoor was the head coach of the women's team and the assistant coach was another of my former coaches, George Haines.

"I don't swim competitively anymore, of course; now I only swim for pleasure. Sailing currently satisfies my need for competition. I also ski and took second place in a giant slalom race when I had only been skiing for about ten days. But there are times when I miss the thrill of swimming competition, especially the glamour and excitement of the Olympics.

"I'm definitely glad it's over, but I think that I'm as satisfied as I am because I went out on top. The seven gold medals count, of course, but what is more important to me is that I did the best I could, and when I finished I was on top.

"So I had no regrets in quitting. I held the world record in everything I swam during the 1972 Olympics and accomplished what to me is the ultimate dream.

"And then again I swam for twelve years, which is a pretty healthy career, and went out at the usual age for men—about twenty-two.

"I do miss the camaraderie I had with all the swimmers, always going to the pool and messing around. Not that I gave up swimming; I just don't train as I used to or anything close to it. But I am in the water a couple of times a week. When I get tired, I get out. I still enjoy swimming and expect I always will."

1 | Making Friends with the Water

SWIMMING IS ESSENTIAL. It should be as basic to a child's education as learning the ABC's. Swimming helps you develop balance, coordination, and confidence. And it is a part of safety education since there may come a time when you would have to know how to swim in order to save your own or someone else's life. Swimming is also good physical exercise and best of all, it's just plain fun. In fact, there are few activities that are as beneficial to you that are as much fun. It is a sport that can be enjoyed by all ages and in all seasons—provided, of course, that you live relatively near an indoor swimming pool and today there are very few of us who don't.

Aside from swimming for its own sake, there are various other sports such as scuba diving, water skiing, sailing, high diving, water polo, and water basketball that would be either dangerous or impossible without knowing how to swim. So learning how to swim is adding pleasure to your life.

Another good thing about swimming is that learning how is not difficult. It is even easier if you have a good instructor and the learning process proceeds in a leisurely, relaxed manner. Above all, you should be as relaxed as possible in the water—whether you are the teacher or the student. This means, of course, that any fear of the water that you feel should be eliminated as soon as possible because it is the greatest handicap to learning how to swim. Fear can originate in the swimmer or it can be passed on to him from the instructor who may feel unnecessarily apprehensive about his student for one reason or another.

The fear of water—in very basic terms—is the fear of going under, of not being able to breathe. When you are afraid, your concentration is broken and your muscles are not able to work properly because you become tense. This results in impaired coordination, both in learning and in the actual physical performance. You cannot keep your body in a constant state of tension or contraction—a state that can be caused by fear. Muscles can only be tensed for a limited period of time before they grow tired. They must be relaxed from time to time in order for them to continue functioning properly.

When fear causes you to lose concentration, your mind is blotting out all helpful incoming stimuli and you can't hear instructions properly—if at all. In order to learn how to swim, you have to be relaxed and be able to concentrate on what the instructor is telling you. Therefore, the first and foremost step in learning how to swim is to erase your fear of water.

Sometimes the fear of water is compounded by the tension caused by water that is too cold. Most of us will hesitate a bit—even if we are good swimmers—before jumping into water that is cold. We tend to tense up, to draw into a knot. This problem should be eliminated, if at all possible, by learning in water that is heated to a good training temperature, between 77 and 80 degrees Fahrenheit. Actually I feel that the perfect training temperature is 80 degrees, for water that is any warmer tends to drain too much energy out of you, and water that is much colder makes you too tense.

I learned to swim with my father when I was about six years old. He taught me to swim underwater first because he felt—and I share the feeling—that the fear of water comes from the desire to stay on top of the water while the natural tendency of the body is to go under. The whole idea of swimming is that you are trying to manipulate yourself in a different environment and so the way to start out properly is to get acquainted with that different environment, to make friends with the water. The best way to make friends is to totally submerge yourself.

When I learned to swim, my family owned a small boat, a 25-foot cabin cruiser. At that time we were living in Sacramento, California. We went to the Stockton Channels, which empty into the San Francisco Bay, and while we were there, my father figured it would be a good time to teach all of us—my two sisters and me—how to swim. We would go out in the Channels often and even after we learned how to swim, I would have to wear a lifejacket, which I completely detested. But the Channels were dangerous because of their strong undercurrents, and my father was right. It is important to remember that the ocean or any other body of water with a strong current is much stronger than any individual and it is best not to get too confident in such water because it will beat you every time.

A swimming pool, or any still body of water, is the best place to learn how to swim. It is essentially a dead body of water and you are in control. In dealing with the ocean or water with a current, you have to constantly deal with its movement. This book will not discuss learning to swim in the ocean or any other moving body of water. It will deal with learning in a pool, so that the only movement you have to worry about is your own.

My father first taught me to swim underwater, which is a pretty simple process. Basically, everyone can hold his breath. Babies do it out of anger. Out of the water, all you have to do when you wish to breathe again is to do so. In the water, it is an entirely different situation. You are confined and in order to breathe you have to do something specific.

This brings up the overall principle of swimming as I see it. Learning to swim is probably the first instance in anybody's life—especially if learning to swim comes at an early age—in which something absolutely *must* be done in order to survive.

If the rigid rules of swimming are not followed, the swimmer will sink and probably drown. In the beginning this simply means that you must hold your breath underwater and when you wish to take another breath, you must rise to the surface. In the meantime, to enjoy yourself underwater, you should learn to propel yourself there.

Learning to propel yourself underwater before you learn to completely relax while holding your breath doesn't make sense. Even though you may get impatient as your skill and confidence in the water increase, you should not be confused by attempting to learn too many things at once. You should master each aspect of the learning process before progressing to the next—no matter how tedious and boring.

Initially you and your instructor should be in water shallow enough so that you can touch bottom. The water should be waist to shoulder high, as long as you feel comfortable. Later in the teaching process, it is advisable to swim in water over your head. Since there is no difference in the feel of deep water as opposed to shallow water (except for the loss of ability to touch bottom), there are no adjustments to be made in moving from the shallow to the deep end of the pool.

The instructor should be someone with whom you feel safe and comfortable, since learning to swim is based on the building of confidence between two people. I had confidence in my father, but I could certainly have felt at ease with another competent instructor.

Once the instructor earns your confidence he should demonstrate everything he asks you to do. In the elementary stages of swimming I don't believe in being told what to do and then following instructions without first watching someone else do it. When you're learning to do something that is new to you, it is always best to have a practical demonstration of what you are attempting to master, even after you have had the process explained.

For example, you learn how to multiply, add, or subtract by watching the teacher demonstrate the process on a blackboard after the teacher has explained it or after studying the process in a book. The combination of explanation and demonstration gives you a better grasp of the principal involved.

Of course, the most important part of the whole learning process is actually doing it yourself. And practicing, practicing, practicing!

After the familiarity has been built up between the student and the instructor, the student should practice holding his breath out of the water. The instructor will show you that you can hold your breath for 20 or 30 seconds out of the water, and then he will tell you that if you can hold your breath for that long out of the water, you can certainly hold your breath underwater for 10 seconds. Provided you are not afraid. Fear takes away your concentration and energy. Relax, have confidence in your instructor, and take the plunge.

You can't be expected at first to hold your breath underwater as long as you can out of the water. And if you are moving you will wind up staying underwater even less time.

What's really pleasant about swimming underwater, you will find, is that it is a completely new environment. Quiet. You are left alone, suspended, almost as if you were experiencing weightlessness. If you have ever seen Dustin Hoffman in *The Graduate*, you will probably remember the scene in which the character Hoffman played in the movie escaped from the social pressure around him by taking to the bottom of the pool. Once you have learned to enjoy the underwater world, you will appreciate how peaceful it can be.

Also, building up confidence by swimming, or at least being able to hold your breath and open your eyes underwater, enables you to relax on top of the water because you won't fear going under. You won't fear to put your face in the water, for you will know what it is like down there, and you will be confident that you will survive.

Swimming underwater is a useful skill to learn for other reasons, too. If you go any place that has a recreational swimming pool, you will find that there is none of this business of swimming laps back and forth. All the swimmers are underwater playing tag.

The initial movements you make while trying to manipulate yourself underwater should be simple ones. But once you have mastered the act of just staying under for a period of time, you should—with the instructor's help—attempt to move about slowly. At this point you will begin to appreciate the buoyancy and the density of the water and you will experience the tendency of your body to rise to the surface as you begin to relax and gain confidence. Of course, all this is very basic. But for a person unfamiliar with water, it is a new and important discovery and an important step toward becoming a good swimmer.

2 | Floating and Other Basic Skills

AFTER YOU HAVE BECOME familiar with the underwater environment and are comfortable in it, the next step in the process is to learn how to float on your back. Learning to float adds to your confidence in the water and helps in understanding the importance of balance.

Basically, all strokes depend on an evenly maintained balance, and when you alter that balance, you will find you have to strain much more than is necessary.

There is an age-old principle that is good to know in understanding swimming: Newton's Third Law of Motion. Every action, Newton formulized, has an equal and opposite reaction. This is true when you are walking or running, for example. If you push with your legs against the ground with 50 pounds of thrust, you will move forward and upward with 50 pounds of thrust. The same is true of swimming. If you grab water with your hand and pull it backward with 20 pounds of thrust, you will be propelling your body through the water with 20 pounds of thrust. (Of course, this is purely theoretical, since the resistance we will speak of later would diminish this thrust.)

Newton's principle applies also to other aspects of swimming, such as balance. In the water your body acts much like a boat. If you were to step into the front of a boat, the rear would rise out of the water as the front went down. If you are floating and you drop your head underwater, the reaction is for your legs to rise, and vice versa. If you place your hands above the head while floating on your back, therefore throwing the weight distribution of the body forward, the reaction is for the legs to rise in the water in order to maintain a balance.

As you read this book you might be thinking, "But his form of swimming can get so technical that I would have to be a genius to understand it." No, of course not. In fact, it is all very simple. Again, example and illustration are important. You can't put some-one in an astronaut's capsule and send him into space without telling him how to experience weightlessness. Nor can you teach someone how to drive a car without familiarizing him with the rela-tionship between the steering wheel and the direction in which the car moves.

Later, when more advanced, you will probably want to learn more about fluid mechanics. There are several swimming books on the market that discuss this topic in greater depth. An excellent book of this kind is Doc (James E.) Counsilman's *The Science of Swimming*.

To return to floating, I think that after you have learned to hold your breath underwater and know how to move about a little, the next step in the learning process should be attempting to float on your back.

I taught a fifty-eight-year-old woman how to float in just a few minutes because she had complete confidence in me. This was another example of the confidence that is so important between the instructor and the student. The woman was already somewhat familiar with the water, but even so, the facility with which she learned was quite remarkable.

She lay completely flat on her back in the water with her legs slightly apart, maybe a foot and a half to two feet maximum, and kept her waist stiff to avoid sagging at the hips. The beginner has a tendency to drop his rear end in the water and since the legs are lighter, they rise to the surface and he winds up in a sitting posi-tion. You'll know what I mean when you give it a try.

In learning how to float on your back, try to consciously keep the waist stiff at all times, but not rigid. If you try too hard to keep yourself stiff while you are floating, you'll drive your legs down and then you've lost the balance you need to float freely.

Your arms should be fully extended over your head, but kept in their natural arc (as when they hang at your sides). It doesn't mat-ter too much if they are so relaxed that your thumbs and palms are very close to your head, but it is preferable that you keep your arms extended so that the hands are at least twelve inches apart. Then as you lie back in the water, consciously think of the waist as being stiff, not bending. Take a deep breath, but do not, and I repeat, *do not,* exhale totally, because the whole principle of floating is that your lungs are filled with enough air to create a float.

If you wish to experiment, exhale totally and you will find that you will sink, just as an inner tube float will sink if you let all the air out.

In the beginning, the instructor should hold you up with his hands placed lightly under your back. When you begin to feel completely relaxed, the instructor should slowly lessen the pressure until the water itself is actually holding you up. The instructor should not remove his hand entirely, though, until you are totally confident.

Once he removes his hand, you should try to remain relaxed, and not allow your rear end to sink in the water. At first, when the instructor begins to remove his hands from your back, you will find yourself following the hand removal with your body and forgetting about the stiffness in the waist. In such an instance, begin over until you are finally floating freely and easily.

If you are relaxed enough, you will be floating. If you are not floating, I will guarantee you that it is because you are bending at the waist, provided that your hands and arms are fully extended over your head in a relaxed position. The legs may have a tendency to float out a bit, but that's okay.

Now, in order to assume a floating position on your own, you need only follow the following steps. First, slowly bring your arms up over your head as you lean back in the water. It is important that your arms be over your head as they will act as a counterbalance to the legs and cause them to rise (per Newton's principle).

The arms are now fully extended, and you should take a deep breath. From now on while floating, you will try to keep your chest at least 50 percent full of air and to keep the body relaxed; it's just relaxed breathing, actually.

You may try to hold your breath completely at first and then slowly exhale—just a small amount at a time and then refill your lungs, but you must always remember to keep the lungs at least half full of air. Now, in the relaxed state, you should try to keep the body straight and flat in the water.

If at this point you wish to experiment, do so. You will find as you let more and more air out of your lungs that you will begin to sink. You will also find that you are sinking the most in your rear end. But if you quickly inhale again and hold your breath, you will slowly rise back to the surface. Another experiment you might try is to bring your arms down toward your head more. The more you bring them down, the more your legs will drop in the water. The only way to compensate for this is to bring your arms slowly forward again and you will feel your legs rising back toward the surface.

By such experimentation, you will start to feel a natural position for yourself in the water. You will begin to relax and enjoy the floating feeling.

The back float is the most valuable float to perfect, as it is used as a resting technique in surface swimming and it is necessary to learn before attempting the back crawl (described in Chapter 5) or any other type of floating, such as the prone float (also known as the dead man's float).

The same principle of filling your lungs with air applies to the prone float, although you will be lying facedown in the water and you won't be breathing in and out. In order to get into the prone float position, simply extend both hands above your head, approximately six or so inches apart, and place your face in the water. It is best that you stand in about chest-deep water. Push off the bottom of the pool with both feet, relax, and let your feet rise toward the surface.

According to your physical makeup, your feet will either rise close to the surface or they will hang in the water in an angled position. You must be totally relaxed, almost as if you were going to drift off to sleep.

In order to stand on the bottom again, bring your knees up under your body and push against the water with your hands. Your body will move into a vertical position and you will be able to stand in the water easily.

If you wish to go from a back float position to a prone float position, simply bend your knees and drop your legs as if you were going to stand, and, using your arms to balance your body, gently let your body swing in an arc until your face comes forward in the water and you can straighten your body out. Simply reverse the process in going from the prone position to the back position.

Another basic maneuver, which is good to learn at this point, is

The back float as seen from below water level. Note the position of the hands and feet, the horizontal position of the body, and the stiffness in the waist.

To change position from the back float to the prone float bring your arms to the sides and drop your body.

Continue the movement by pushing down against the water with the hands and tucking the knees up against the body.

Almost in the prone float position, the arms and hands extend forward, the body straightens, and the feet push backward in the water.

The prone float position is reached. The arms are extended in front of the head approximately six inches apart and the body is relaxed.

treading water. Although treading water is a form of dog paddling, it can be a very advanced technical process.

Your body is vertical in the water with your head remaining above it. Your feet will probably be moving although it is not absolutely necessary to maintain this position. If the legs are moved back and forth in a flutter kick, it will relieve some of the pressure from the hands and the arm movement can be slower, more relaxed.

The basic thing to remember is the placement of the hands in relation to the water. The arms should be in a horizontal plane with the bottom of the pool, but the hands should be turned in a 45-degree angle to the bottom. Your arms moving constantly back and forth with your hands always at this angle is a technique called sculling. The palms will be facing outward when you move them away from the body; as you bring them back, you must turn the palms inward toward the body.

Treading water is an important skill to learn, for it enables you to rest, change strokes, and look around to get your bearings in the water. It is also an enjoyable skill, for it will let you stand still in the water and talk to friends. It takes very little effort on your part and

Treading water is an important skill to learn, for it enables you to rest, change strokes, and get your bearings in the water.

The basic thing to remember while sculling is the placement of the hands. They should be horizontal to the bottom of the pool, with the palms at a 45-degree angle as they move in and out in front of the body.

with a little practice you will find yourself becoming quite adept at it.

Now you should know how to float on your back and on your stomach and how to tread water. It is time we learned some simple, basic gliding maneuvers. However, let me reemphasize that in learning any basic stroke there should be an instructor with you at all times. Even if the water is only chest deep, there should be someone at your side who knows how to swim.

Let's begin with the front glide. Since you already know the prone float, this will be very simple for you. From a standing position, bend at the waist, take a deep breath, and bring your legs up toward the surface of the water, allowing them to touch the side of the pool, and push off from there. You may also push yourself off

The feet move back and forth in a flutter kick which will take some of the pressure from the hand and arm movement.

from the bottom of the pool in either deep or shallow water, but in the beginning it is easier if you use the side. How far and how fast your glide will carry you depends upon the strength of your push-off and how long you can hold your breath. When you feel it is time to take another breath, tuck your knees up under your body, push down against the water with your hands, and allow your body to swing into a vertical position as your face comes out of the water for a breath. You will find your feet touching bottom. If not, simply go into the treading-water maneuver which you have already learned.

After you are fairly proficient in gliding through the pool and you feel comfortable doing so, it is time to add a flutter kick to the glide. You can do this simply by moving your legs back and forth

(LEFT): The forward glide can be performed underwater as well as on the surface. First bend your knees and extend your arms above the head.

(MIDDLE): Push off from the bottom, fully extending the body and keeping the head tucked between your arms.

(RIGHT): To continue the forward movement at this point you could add a flutter kick or any of the leg and arm movements covered in the following chapters.

in the water, keeping the knees taut, and moving only from the hips. While the ankles need to be relaxed, your toes should be pointed. Your knees will bend slightly on the down thrust, so you should not keep them *too* stiff. Be conscious of the fact that the basic movement should come at the hip, so that the whole leg moves up and down; not merely the part from the knee to the foot.

You may wish to practice the kick before attempting to use it with the front glide. To do so, simply hold on to the side of the pool, take a deep breath, place your face in the water, bring your legs out behind you and kick, using the movement described above. Your feet should not break the surface of the water. After you have gained confidence and ease of movement, you will want to push off from the side and propel yourself by this kicking action as far as you can across the pool. The instructor should be watching you to see that you keep your knees properly stiff and that the other aspects of your movement are correct.

You will find that it is fairly easy to change direction in the water. Simply turn your head in the direction you wish to swim. Once you have mastered the crawl, a sharper turn can be executed by reaching in the new direction with the stroking arm.

Up to this point, it is likely that you have entered the water by jumping into the shallow end, or you have used the ladder to lower yourself in. But now you are ready to make your first dive. This is

In order to change direction while in the water, reach with your hand in the direction you wish to go, and allow the rest of your body to follow.

actually a feet-first dive. Walk to the edge of the pool and step off into the water just as if you were completing a step upon a solid surface. As you enter the water, keep your hands at your sides a little away from the body so that they will catch the water and keep you from going too deep. Once you have entered the water, begin at once to climb your way back to the surface, much as if you were climbing a ladder; this movement with the hands and feet will bring you up to the surface very quickly and you may begin treading water.

At this point in your instruction, perhaps this is the only dive you should use from the edge of the pool, although illustrations of simple head-first dives can be found in Chapter Eight. There are also two dives you may wish to learn that can be attempted while

The weight of the legs above the water will force the body downward.

The body is streamlined with both hands and feet together, and the body is pointed directly toward the bottom of the pool.

Another surface dive you can learn is called the pike surface dive. To accomplish this dive, take a deep breath, place yourself in the prone float position, and when you are ready, bend your body sharply at the waist, forcing your head down into the water and your hips up out of the water. At the same time bring your legs up. This, according to Newton's theory, should force your head even further down into the water. You can help to submerge your body deeper into the water by pushing up with your hands against the

On reaching the desired depth, bring the hands back toward the hips, pushing against the water to bring your body parallel to the bottom of the pool, and start swimming.

water. Pull your body into a horizontal position with your arms and you're ready to swim or glide. To get a breath, follow the same procedure as before.

Your eyes should open at all times while you are underwater. It is a part of your safety while swimming to be able to see where you are going, and you will find when you are used to it that it adds immeasurably to your swimming pleasure.

3 | The Sidestroke and Elementary Backstroke

AT THIS POINT in your lessons you should feel fairly confident in the water. You have learned to float, glide, tread water, and to feel at ease when totally submerged. You are actually ready to learn the crawl stroke, although you may wish to learn two very simple strokes first—the sidestroke and the elementary backstroke.

The sidestroke and the elementary backstroke are the easiest strokes to perform since they do not require you to learn a breathing technique. Your face remains above water at all times and you are free to breathe whenever it is comfortable for you to do so. With their slow, deliberate movements, both strokes are also useful as resting strokes. In addition, the sidestroke is important to know if you plan to study lifesaving techniques.

The sidestroke is, of course, performed with the swimmer lying on his side. Although either side is fine to use, a right-handed swimmer usually lies on his right side and a left-handed swimmer on his left.

The kick used with the sidestroke is called the scissors kick. The kick is executed by drawing your knees up to just under the level of your hips, keeping the legs together. Then bring the bottom leg backward and the top leg forward as if you were going to take a step. As your legs reach the end of their movement apart, bring them back together again, just as if you were closing a pair of scissors.

The kick must be coordinated with the arm movement, described as follows: Your body will be lying on your side with the arm on top resting against your body, palm down. The bottom arm should be fully extended in front of you in the water. The legs at this point should be together, fully extended behind you. Your body is in a modified glide position.

Now with the bottom arm, which is extended in front of you, grab the water and bring the arm down toward the bottom of the pool until it is directly below your ear. Then bend the arm at the elbow, bringing the hand directly up toward the ear, keeping the hand in a straight up and down position to minimize drag in the water. As the hand reaches up toward the ear, the movement then should be to recover the arm, returning it to the original position, knifing the hand through the water.

The movement of the arm on top should be synchronized with the movement of the bottom arm. As the bottom arm is grabbing water and starting down toward the bottom of the pool, the top arm will begin a movement forward reaching (with the elbow bent) toward the hand that will be approaching the ear. Just at the point that the bottom hand has reached up toward the ear with the palm pointed forward ready to knife through the water to the original position, the top hand will also be near the face, as if in a clapping position—the difference being that the palms are not facing each other. The palm of the bottom arm will be facing out away from the face, and the palm of the top arm will be facing down toward the bottom of the pool. Then as the bottom arm reaches back in the water toward the original position, the top arm begins its thrust stroke. From the chin position, the hand grabs water and pushes it back toward the hips, sweeping in an arc until it returns to the original position.

A scissors kick should be made with each arm stroke, the legs being the greatest distance apart just at the moment when the hands are in a clapping position. They return to the original starting position at the same point the hands do. The important thing to remember about the kick, is that the bottom leg moves backward and the top leg moves forward.

In performing this stroke, your head is out of the water at all times, so there is no wrong time to breathe. You may breathe at any time that makes you feel comfortable. Naturally, you will find yourself breathing, stroking, and kicking in a steady rhythm after you have become proficient at this stroke.

In the sidestroke, the hands and feet never break the surface of the water. The movements are performed in a leisurely, relaxed manner.

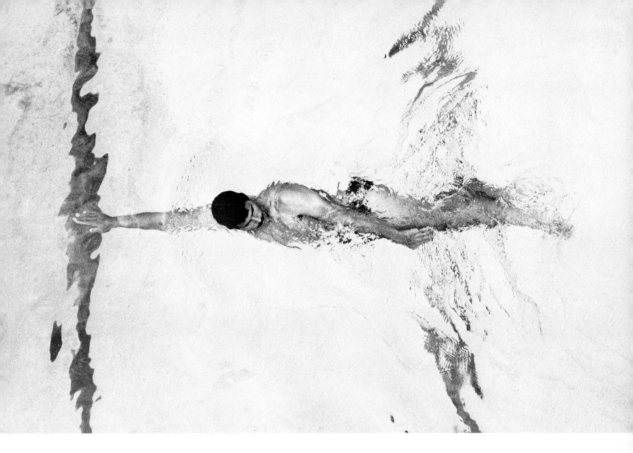

The starting position of the sidestroke as seen from above and below the surface of the water. Note the positions of the hands and feet.

The bottom arm (extended in front) grabs water and starts to come back while the top hand reaches forward.

The hands near each other in a semiclapping position and the legs begin the scissors kick with the bottom leg going to the back, and the top leg toward the front.

Notice that the hands and feet never break the surface of the water. The hands begin to move away from each other as the legs continue to move apart.

The bottom arm reaches over the head while the top arm pushes back.
The legs have reached their apogee and will begin to move back together,
the action which results in most of the forward propulsion.

In performing the stroke, the head is out of the water at all times, so there is no wrong time to breathe. The feet whip back together.

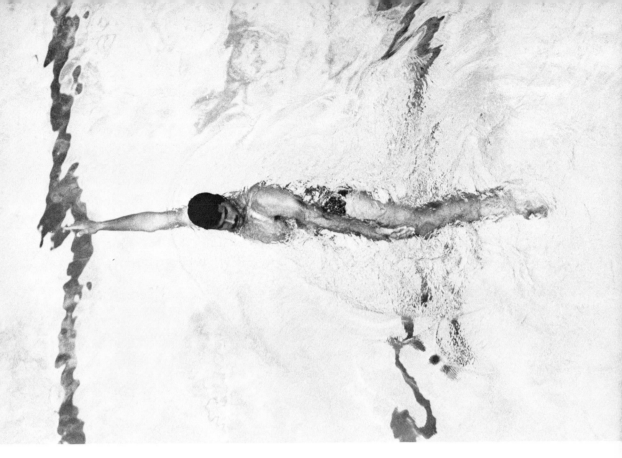

Back in the starting position. Generally, the movements in the sidestroke are performed in a leisurely, relaxed manner. It is a resting stroke.

The elementary backstroke is performed while lying on the back. Since you have already learned how to float on your back, this stroke should present no problem for you. At the outset your legs are together and fully extended from the body. The arms should be resting at your side.

The kick used is the frog kick. As you are lying on your back, bring your feet up an imaginary center line of your body toward your hips, keeping the heels together. Your knees will be out away from each other in a position similar to that of a frog's legs. When the legs reach up toward the hips as far as they can go, the feet should then be pushed down and out from the body while the legs are brought together. This causes a strong whiplike action.

As the legs are brought up toward the hips with the feet together, the hands begin their movement back toward the head. The elbows bend and the palms are turned so that the edges of the palms are parallel to the surface of the pool. The hands should not break the surface of the water. Just as the hands reach shoulder level, the legs will come up toward the center line of the body, reaching the frog's legs' position. At the same time that the hands grab water at the shoulder level and push down toward the original position alongside the body, the legs will push down with the kick. Both the leg action and arm action are performed simultaneously. The body will glide through the water while the arms and legs are once again moving into position for the kick and stroke.

The elbows remain stiff during the arm stroke. They are bent only during the recovery of the stroke.

We mentioned that the arms should not break the surface of the water at any time. That is also true of the legs. The main problem with the legs breaking the surface of the water is that they would tend to push a wave of water toward the swimmer's face, which would cause problems with the swimmer's breathing.

The elementary backstroke begins with the feet together and hands at the sides.

As the legs are brought up toward the hips with the feet together, the hands begin their movement back toward the head.

The elbows bend and the palms begin to turn so that the edges will be parallel to the surface of the pool. The heels near the hips.

The kick used is called the frog kick. Note the position of the feet and hands and that they are moved simultaneously at all times.

When the legs have reached up toward the hips as far as they can go, they are pushed down and out from the body as the legs are brought together.

At exactly the same time that the legs kick down, the hands at shoulder level grab water and push down toward the original position.

The body is back in the original position and will glide through the water as the arms and legs are moving into the stroke and kick position again.

4 | The Crawl

YOU ARE NOW READY to begin your lessons in earnest, starting with the basic stroke—the crawl. The crawl is usually referred to as the freestyle stroke, but for the sake of clarity it will be called the crawl here.

Since you have already learned to feel confident in the water and not to be afraid of submerging your face, you will be able to learn the proper techniques of this stroke, including the correct way to breathe. Proper breathing technique is very important if you ever plan to pursue competitive swimming. As you will see later, breathing correctly will help you maintain the balance that is so essential to swimming with the least effort and the greatest speed.

Swimming requires a tremendous amount of coordination and balance. For example, in the crawl stroke, each hand moves independently. And in theory, at least, when one hand is in front of you, then the other hand is in back to keep your balance. The arms work in the manner of a windmill.

But in practice this is not always true. The reason is simply because water is denser than air. The arm moving in the air moves faster than the arm moving in the water, so the arms are not always in the perfect theoretical balance.

Perhaps this is as good a place as any to re-introduce some fluid mechanics. It is easy to understand that if you have a piece of board which measures two feet by one foot by two inches the easiest way to move it through the water would be to lay it flat in the water. The rate of speed at which the board will move will depend on how fast the board is being pulled through the water and what resistance the two-inch surface causes the speed to diminish. In actual fact, of course, there is more resistance than just the two-inch surface pushing against the water (which is called frontal resistance); there is also a resistance caused by the water flowing past the flat surface of the board (which is called surface resistance) and by the turbulence at the back of the board formed by the water rushing past the surface of the board (which is called eddy resistance). All of this resistance causes the forward speed of the board to lessen, and if any of these three resistances were increased (for instance, if the board were tilted so that the surface area causing frontal resistance were greater) then the speed would diminish even more.

The same principles apply to the human body while swimming. Of course, the body surface is much more complicated and there are more aspects of fluid mechanics to worry about than with the flat piece of board. But one thing is the same: the flatter the body is in relation to the surface of the water, the less resistance and therefore the less drag there will be to cut down on your rate of swimming speed.

When the body is the most streamlined in the water, it is in the most perfect balance, and basically in all strokes the body must be in balance. When you alter that balance, you will find that you have to strain more, for you have more drag to overcome.

Beginners tend to become frustrated easily while swimming and they have a constant feeling that they are going to sink. Out of fear, they have a tendency to lift their heads up to take more of a breath, because they feel they are not getting enough air. When they do lift their heads, they force their legs deeper into the water and work harder to keep moving, becoming more frightened and eventually panicking. They also kick harder, without knowing the techniques of kicking. They will find that they are expending needless energy moving in no direction and they are dragging themselves deeper and deeper into the water to where they are almost in a vertical position. They are then thrashing. They have lost all control of their balance. They are no longer swimming in any sense, for the coordination and balance that are the basis of swimming have been totally lost.

Coordination and balance will come only when the pupil relaxes. Relaxation, coordination, and balance are three of the essentials of swimming.

Of the four basic strokes used in competitive swimming (the crawl, the breaststroke, the butterfly, and the backstroke), the most adaptable and the most efficient in terms of energy expended is the crawl. It is also the fastest stroke when it is employed properly.

We mentioned earlier that the crawl is often referred to as the freestyle. At one time the crawl was one of the competitive races and in it you had to use the crawl stroke. Now, however, they have changed the name of the event to the freestyle, and the rules are such that you can swim any stroke you wish, provided that you employ the same stroke throughout the race. You can't change strokes in mid-pool.

Since there is no longer an event called the crawl, even though the stroke most often employed in the freestyle event is the crawl, the name changed. However, as we mentioned earlier, to avoid confusion between the competitive event and the type of stroke, we will stick to the old label and call it the crawl stroke.

In performing the crawl, if the swimmer is viewed from above, it appears that he is crawling like a baby, reaching out with one hand at a time. The crawl is probably derived from the so-called dog paddle where the swimmer kicks his legs and moves his hands as a dog would move his paws while swimming in the water.

Dogs do not instinctively know how to swim. It has been proven that dogs, when first introduced to the water, will—out of fear— start to run. And they find that their hind legs tire more rapidly than do their front legs. When the back legs get tired, the dog draws his hind legs up to his stomach and his front paws continue moving. It is at this point that a dog starts to propel himself forward, as opposed to the previous thrashing movements when the back legs were also kicking and the dog was getting nowhere.

Everything was working against everything else. However, when the dog did tire and his back legs were tucked up under him, or just allowed to hang limp behind him, he began to propel himself forward.

So it is with a beginning swimmer. He learns through his bad experiences or through just plain fatigue. Unfortunately, a human doesn't have the type of drive that a dog has when he is learning to swim. And if the human gets tired, he simply stands up—provided he is in shallow water.

Therefore I think it is essential—under close supervision, of course—that after you become familiar with the water, and have learned to be comfortable in it, you should be taught to swim in water above your head. Then you won't be tempted to take "the out" of standing up when you get tired or flustered.

Again, example and illustration are very important; if the instructor tells the beginner why he should do something and then demonstrates, the beginner will be more apt to do the exercise correctly when he begins to practice it himself. As an example, the instructor might use the story of the dog to show him that his feet sometimes—if improperly used—will tend to drag him down in the water, and he gets tired with all the fruitless effort, both with his legs and arms. He will also find that if he will just relax, as the dog did out of sheer exhaustion, he can swim without using his legs at all.

It is true that in competitive swimming if the swimmer does not kick his legs and pulls with his arms he will create a different balance ratio and he will have less power. In competitive swimming, the harder you kick the faster you go.

A beginner can very slowly move his arms in a rhythmic pattern and his legs will almost automatically take up the slack in his balance ratio and begin to kick in rhythm to his arm strokes, thereby restoring the balance.

For example, if in the water a swimmer lifts his right arm, he has a tendency to also lift his right leg and push his left leg down, kicking to keep his balance. If the swimmer just lets his legs go limp, he will find that as he begins to take strokes with his arms, his legs, just from rocking back and forth, will tend to make up the balance difference automatically.

It is a well-worn cliché that when a good swimmer starts to loaf and begins to relax more—just going through the motions—he will find that he doesn't kick. He will do whatever he has to do to propel himself forward, but with the least amount of effort. And the first thing he will stop doing is kicking.

So we will leave the specifics of kicking until later, and for now tend to let the legs find their own rhythm in the total pattern of the crawl stroke.

To begin the crawl, you will be lying flat in the water facedown. In the beginning, we will talk about a center line, an imaginary line drawn down your body cutting it neatly in half—left side from right.

The arm is fully extended forward and enters the water with approximately the same curvature as when hanging at your side.

The basic principle of the crawl, or any stroke for that matter, is to move the arm from point A to point B down the imaginary center line of your body. At the beginning of the stroke cycle, the swimmer has one arm extended out in front of his head and the other arm down at his side, parallel to his thigh.

If you stand at attention, your thumbs will hit a specific spot on your thighs. If an imaginary piece of tape is placed at this point you will find that when you pull your left arm from its forward position above your head, down the imaginary center line, back to your leg, your thumb will touch the tape mark on your thigh. The other arm follows the same procedure on the other side of the body in a windmill effect as you move through the water. Each arm reaches forward to grab new water and pulls straight back down the center line to pass the tape point and then recover out of the water and so on.

During this pulling process, the arm should remain straight—but not totally straight, unless that is the nature of your arm. Everybody's arm is of a different length and everybody's arm feels more comfortable at a different curvature.

For example, when I stand normally, my arms are not naturally straight. They have a slight natural curve to them. When I swim and my arms are trying to drive down a center line, my hand definitely follows down that line, but my arm isn't perfectly straight.

In order to utilize more of your muscle power and to provide more strength in your thrust, it is best to allow your arm to remain in its natural curvature.

During this pulling stroke the hands should be semicupped with the fingers slightly apart. It is not necessary to close the fingers, or to force the hands into a closed-cup effect. It has been proven in wind tunnel tests that an open hand and a closed hand have equal surface areas for pulling and that a relaxed palm is better for swimming. It allows the swimmer to be more at ease, under less tension, and it also allows him to "feel" or know the water. It is important as well as enjoyable to develop a "feel" for the water, because it permits more maneuverability in coping with various situations. Most good swimmers have a feel for the water.

After the arm has entered the water, you should be concentrating on keeping your forearm and the palm of your hand as close to the center line of your body as possible—and don't bend your wrists. There is a tremendous amount of water that you are moving with the palm of your hand and if the wrist "slips," or bends, you start to "slip the water" since you don't have enough surface area to pull the water. In order to maintain your pulling power it is important to keep your wrists straight during the pulling part of your stroke.

The whole idea of maneuvering in swimming is to move water. The more water you can grab in each stroke and actually move, the greater your propulsion. Let's say that the distance between the point at which your hand enters the water to the point your hand leaves is four feet, measuring in a straight line on the surface of the water. If it takes exactly ten seconds to pull that far, you would be pulling four feet of water in ten seconds.

In actual swimming, however, the hand does not move in a straight line. If it did, quite a bit of cavitation would develop behind the palm of the hand. Cavitation is composed of the air bubbles and turbulence that whirl up when the pulling process begins. Since this is not "clean," or turbulence-free, water, the swimmer must change the pitch of his stroking hand several times during a stroke. You will find as you develop your stroke, you will want to change the pitch of your hand every time the turbulence starts. In doing so you are actually moving a greater amount of water over a greater distance than if your hand remained in one position. What's more, you are constantly grabbing clean water, with no turbulence to cause additional drag. These two elements give you more propulsion, and therefore you can swim much faster.

Keep pulling this way until your hand is exactly perpendicular to your torso. At this point, if you were to continue back with your forearm, wrist, and upper arm in the same position you would find that you would be pushing the water upward and actually forcing your body down into the water.

Instead, there are two new angles introduced here. I don't want to get too technical, but you must get your arm out of the water with the least amount of drag, and recover your stroke to its starting position in front of your head.

The stroking arm is seen here following the imaginary center line of the body. The elbow is bent at this point.

When your arm is perpendicular to your torso, bend the elbow so that the forearm and the upper arm form a sharp angle, and the palm is lifted forward so that it, too, forms a sharp angle. Now when you lift your arm out of the water, your upper arm and forearm are almost at water level and the palm of the hand will come cleanly out of the water instead of pushing the water back as it would have done.

The beginning of the arm stroke is seen here from above. The arm is fully extended, ready to enter the water.

Keeping the thumb and palm as close to the body as you can, reach forward. The arm is now in a relaxed state; it is extended forward in position to begin the process all over again.

The right arm is performing exactly the mirror image of what your left arm has just completed—approximately 180 degrees behind it.

When the arm is at the back of the stroke, with the thumb touching the thigh at the imaginary tape point we discussed earlier and is ready to begin the recovery of the stroke out of the water, it is much easier to implement the recovery if the opposite shoulder is rotated so that it is deeper in the water. That means the shoulder on the side making the recovery stroke is up out of the water. This positioning of the shoulders facilitates two movements. First, it becomes easier for your arm, which is beginning a new stroke, to reach deeper into the water and grab with more power. You are using more of your back muscles to pull your arm forward. With the added strength of your back muscles and your deeper reach into the water you are getting a greater propulsion.

Secondly, this rotation of the shoulders makes the recovery movement easier and more comfortable. The shoulder does not have to be lifted as high in order for the arm making the recovery to clear the water, and when the arm doing the pulling stroke finishes, the other arm is ready to begin the next stroke, thereby keeping a steady pulling rhythm going.

Our next concern is to coordinate the breathing with the arm stroke. At one time, the old-style Johnny Weismuller (of Tarzan fame) type of breathing was used. This breathing method probably developed as a result of people's hesitancy to put their faces in the water and from their desire to see where they were going. Since their faces were already raised forward, all they had to do to take a breath was to lift their heads high enough to get their mouths out of the water.

This method of breathing is very tiring and causes unnecessary strain on the neck muscles. In essence, what happens is that every time the head is lifted, the feet sink further into the water and cause a drag.

As we mentioned earlier, the body behaves like a balance while it is in the water. If you are perfectly balanced while lying on your stomach in the water, you can actually float high enough to get your nose out of the water. If you lift your head up, you will find that your feet will sink. When you put your head back into the water your feet will rise again.

Breathing in swimming is strictly for survival and in no other way helps the swimming process. It is not necessary to raise your head to look and see where you are going. Today most people do not swim in murky water. And most everyone has the ability to sense when he is going straight.

If you are not going straight, it is because you are favoring one arm over another, and pulling harder with that arm—similar to a car with one wheel turning faster than the others; the car will tend to go in circles.

As for seeing where you are going, you can look to the side and judge where you are in relation to the side of the pool. In a lake

The left arm bends and creates a sharp angle as the thumb and palm are kept as close to the body as possible, reaching forward.

At this point, the body rolls and the head moves to the side with the eyes looking at the side of the pool; you can judge if you are going straight.

When the right arm is at the back of the stroke, with the thumb touching the thigh, the mouth is out of the water for inhalation.

Then when your right arm passes in front of your eyes, you will turn your head to where your chin is on your chest again.

As the arm reaches down to grab new water, the shoulders rotate, which facilitates the lower arm's reaching deeper into the water.

down in the water. At that time, your leg is rather stiff (knee, hip, thigh, and calf are all in a straight line). Kick your leg down during the time your shoulder is down. As you complete the recovery stroke with the left arm and it enters the water to begin the pull, your body rotates in the opposite direction.

The right leg should now be kicking up, and the left leg should be kicking down as the left arm reaches deep into the water to begin its pull.

As you kick down, most of the force should come from the muscles in the thigh. Never stiffen your ankle—it should remain flexible. As you kick down, the top of your foot will push the water down; as you come back up, your relaxed ankle will point downward creating less surface area and less drag. As you can see, if the foot and ankle are at a 90-degree angle to the leg there is less surface to drag water.

If you were to keep your foot and ankle in a stiff position as you kicked down there would be no difference from the relaxed state. You would get thrust, but when you kicked back up, you would also get thrust and go nowhere. Your legs would be merely going up and down in the water. The remedy is to relax the foot and ankle. The water pushing up will force the foot back, creating the surface area for thrust, and the water pushing down on the recovery will cause the toes to point and create less surface area.

In the crawl stroke the legs kick independently of one another, moving naturally once you establish a coordinated, rhythmic pattern of stroking with the arms. The legs will kick down and back as needed to keep the entire body in balance.

The strength of your kick does not necessarily depend on the size of your feet. Of course, the larger your feet, the larger the paddle you have to work with. Yet I have small feet and I am regarded as having a powerful kicking stroke.

As you are moving forward you will find you are thrusting down with the leg for the forward propulsion of the water. It is also true that you get some thrust forward with the recovery kick, but it is not as evident with the crawl kick. It is more evident with the kick that accompanies the butterfly (called the dolphin kick). The whole process of the kick propulsion is called the modulation of water. Due to the nature of the dolphin kick, you will find you get a thrust up in the water as well as down in the water, but more about that later.

In competitive swimming, it is extremely easy to swim the crawl very slowly. It is also easy to swim the backstroke and the breast-stroke very slowly, but you cannot swim the butterfly slowly, just from the nature of the stroke itself. In any case, you should not try to swim the other strokes until you have built up your confidence and coordination by first feeling comfortable underwater, learning how to float, and mastering the crawl stroke.

After you have mastered the essentials of the crawl (and later the butterfly, backstroke, and breaststroke) you should attempt to swim the stroke underwater. You will find that the same techniques of swimming the crawl at the water's surface will apply to swimming completely submerged.

You will also find that it is a lot easier to swim the stroke the right way underwater than it is to alter it. Underwater you will find a lot more resistance to the recovery portion of the crawl, but if you try to change the recovery stroke in any way, you will have a lot more surface area creating more of a drag. It will offset your balance tremendously.

In the crawl each hand moves independently. In theory, when one hand is in front, the other hand is in back to maintain a balance.

The hands, when grabbing water, are kept in a normal, semicupped shape, with the fingers apart. It is not necessary to close the fingers.

It is best to allow the arm to retain its natural curvature rather than force it to be as straight as possible; this provides a stronger thrust.

The kick must be thought of as independent of the arm stroke. The kicking must come naturally if swimming is to be done effortlessly. Here we see the full extension of the arm entering the water.

There is a tremendous amount of water being moved by the palm of the stroking hand so it is important to keep the wrists straight during the pull.

At this point in the pull, the elbow must bend to create a sharp angle, otherwise the water would be pushed upward, forcing the body down.

When the body is most streamlined in the water, its weight is the most evenly balanced, causing the least amount of drag.

Experimenting with the strokes underwater will enable you to get the total feeling of the stroke you are performing. You will feel the balance in a more pronounced way. You will understand the necessity of coordination and relaxation and you will be able to get the total overall feel of the water while performing the strokes. All this will add to your confidence in the water.

Perhaps you're thinking, "Of course he can feel confident in the water; he's the best swimmer in the world." Well, I was no better swimmer than you at one time. I also had to learn.

5 | The Backstroke

THE BACKSTROKE, or back crawl as it is sometimes called, bears a close resemblance to the basic crawl stroke. However, it is not nearly as powerful or as fast a stroke as the front crawl since the arms are in an awkward position when doing the pulling, and cannot apply the same degree of muscle strength to the pull.

To begin the backstroke, you should be lying on your back in the water. It is here that your previous lessons in which you learned to float on your back will come in handy, and you should at this point have progressed to the degree of proficiency where you can comfortably lie in the water and float without sagging in the middle. Your waist will be stiff and your arms extended back over your head. Your legs will be extended down and separated by about a foot. If you can do this comfortably and with confidence, you are ready to begin the backstroke.

The backstroke has a kick that is similar to the crawl kick. It is a flutter kick and each leg performs exactly the opposite of the other. Again, you do not consciously have to think about the kick, for it is a movement that will come naturally to counteract the movement of the arms. As in the crawl, the ankles are kept extremely flexible and the kick is just a thrust down and a thrust back up, accomplished by moving the thighs up and down.

The primary difference between the backstroke kick and the crawl kick is found in the fact that the main thrust in the backstroke kick comes from the upstroke, the reverse of the crawl kick. The knees are bent when the legs are making the upward kick and are kept as straight as possible when the kick is down.

The arms in the backstroke are moved asymmetrically as in the crawl, rotated backward. We will begin the backstroke with the left hand.

Lie on your back in the water with your right arm fully extended along the side of the body with the thumb touching the thigh and the left arm and hand extended over the head and resting with the palm up on the surface of the water. As the left arm starts the pull, the thumb is pointing in toward the imaginary center line of the body, but just as the hand is about to enter the water, the palm is rotated so that the thumb points up toward the sky and the palm enters the water sideways.

The arm should retain its natural curvature during the stroke.

In the crawl, you took a breath as you rolled the right shoulder up and took a stroke with the left arm. As you stroke in the backstroke with the left arm, the right shoulder again rolls up and you can take a breath at this time. Rolling the right shoulder up enables you to get the left shoulder and arm deeper into the water as well as facilitating a cleaner recovery with the right arm. Lifting the right shoulder does not require you to raise the right arm very high to clear the surface of the water. The amount of roll down into the water from the surface plane is approximately four inches or an angle of 45 degrees.

Try to develop a set pattern for your breathing as it is sometimes possible for a backstroke swimmer to breathe too much and breathe too shallowly. If you wish, time your breaths with the same arm stroke pattern as you do when swimming the front crawl.

As you are pulling with your left arm in the backstroke, you will find there will come a time when the arm is approximately in the same horizontal plane as your shoulders. You must now bend the elbow a little bit, which is similar to that described in the freestyle, to complete the stroke. This bending lets your arm continue moving backward until it nears the waist. At that time, flex your wrist a bit and actually whip the water. Besides providing thrust, this enables you to bring your hand out of the water cleanly.

To run through that again: Bring your left arm back over your head with your palm up. The back of your hand is resting on the surface of the water, and your thumb is rotated upward. The palm of your hand slices into the water sideways and the left shoulder drops. The arm begins the pull downward and as it extends straight out and down from the shoulder the elbow bends, continu-

The pulling hand should be approximately in the same horizontal plane as the shoulders.

The elbow bends a bit in order to complete the stroke.

ing the pulling motion by actually pushing the water back. The arm nears the waist and as it does, the wrist should snap down. You then lift your left shoulder up, rolling the right shoulder down into the water. The right arm is already extended up over the head and is ready to begin the alternate stroke.

The left arm recovers directly over your head in the same pattern the right followed when the left arm was stroking. It is recovered directly over your head with a straight arm action as opposed to the recovery in the crawl which used a bent elbow. In the backstroke recovery, the wrist is relaxed on the straight arm. And as the arm comes back over the head, the muscle of the arm should come in very close to the head. As the arm bends down and then relaxes on the water, the thumb should be pointing up. The shoulder rolls down once more and the arm retains its natural curve and pulls all

69

the way through to the whip when the body rolls back to a level position.

You must always remember to roll the hips at the same time and in the same degree as you roll the shoulders. If you roll the shoulders only and keep the hips straight, you will tend to wriggle through the water in a snakelike pattern, and you will find it more difficult to fit your leg kicks into the overall rhythm of the stroke.

You will find if you develop a natural, even arm stroke and you roll your shoulders and hips in a natural (but not too deep) roll, the leg action will fit in snugly with the overall pattern.

The main fault usually found with swimmers of the backstroke is that they tend to sit down in the water. This doesn't work, as it creates too much of a drag. It is true that you must be deep enough in the water to avoid causing unnecessary turbulence at the surface of the water with your flutter kick, but even so your body must remain straight and the waist stiff. For the swimmer who has already learned to float in the proper manner, this should not be a problem.

Remember to keep your chin on your chest and try not to roll your head from side to side every time you take a stroke. The body tends to follow the direction in which the head is pointing. If the head is kept straight, you are more likely to swim straight.

Also remember to keep your chin on your chest and try not to roll your head from side to side every time you take a stroke. The head, in rolling back and forth, throws the swimmer off-balance and makes him dizzy. The body also tends to follow the direction in which the head is pointing. If it is possible, the swimmer should wear a neck brace so that the head will not move. In swimming, the head is functional solely for breathing and for nothing else. The

The arms in the backstroke are moved asymmetrically as in the crawl, only this time they are rotated in a backward fashion.

The backstroke utilizes the flutter kick in which each leg moves exactly opposite the other.

As the right hand begins the stroke (the left is recovering) the body is rolled, enabling the right arm to reach deeper into the water.

The ankles are kept extremely flexible during the kick. The kicking action itself is just a thrust down and a thrust back up.

breaststroke is the only stroke in which the head should be lifted in order to take a breath.

The pattern followed by the arms when they are pulling from the top of the stroke to the point of recovery varies with each individual. However, most swimmers tend to follow an "S" type of pattern in the water, with the hand reaching its deepest point in the water about midway in the stroke (when the arm is straight out from the shoulder) and again at the hips when recovery begins.

Also, in performing this and any other stroke the same change of pitch in the hands during the pulling action should occur as was described in the crawl stroke. When the cavitation builds up behind the palm of the hand, the pitch should change so that you can rid yourself of the turbulence, or dirty water, and can grab new, clean water to increase the power of your pull.

The arm will retain its natural curvature as it strokes. At this point the left arm is beginning the stroke and the right is starting to recover.

Just as the hand beginning the pull enters the water, the palm is rotated so that the palm enters the water sideways.

With the palm reaching back to grab water, the left shoulder is rolled down, enabling the hand to reach deeper into the water.

The primary difference between the backstroke kick and the crawl kick is that the main thrust in the backstroke kick is in the upstroke.

The knees are bent when the legs make the upward kick and are kept as straight as possible when the kick is down.

Note in the backstroke that the wrist on the recovering arm is relaxed once it passes the waist.

6 | The Breaststroke

THE BREASTSTROKE IS a very relaxing stroke. It is also an easy stroke to use when swimming underwater since both the arm and leg actions are performed completely underwater anyway. According to the rules of competitive swimming, you are not allowed to recover out of the water. In most of the other strokes the recovery is out of the water.

The butterfly developed when swimmers began recovering the arm stroke in the breaststroke out of the water and changed the frog kick to the dolphin kick. Both the breaststroke and the butterfly demand exacting coordination to be swum really well. But the butterfly is much more difficult to perform due to the tremendous amount of energy expended.

Although the butterfly is one of my favorite strokes, the breaststroke didn't come easily for me. It may have been because the flexibility in my ankles wasn't quite that of a champion breaststroker. Such physical limitations affect all swimmers to a certain degree. A champion breaststroker, for example, may not have the strength or flexibility in his legs, arms, or back of a champion butterfly swimmer and therefore not excel in that particular stroke. Even though these strokes are similar, each requires slightly different physical characteristics in a swimmer.

I mentioned that the breaststroke is swum with all but the head underwater. There is always resistance in any stroke, but only in the breaststroke does the arm recovery as well as the stroke meet this resistance. To proceed you must take the line of least resistance through the entire execution of the stroke. And I think the feeling of having to move slowly just didn't appeal to me.

Also, the ability just wasn't there. You have to realize you can't have ability in everything—not exceptional ability, anyway.

In the crawl, the kicking and the arm stroke are independent of one another even though once you develop a natural rhythm and balance, the kicking will fall right into place. The kick is also taught independently of the arm action in the backstroke and the butterfly. When you have learned to do the stroke and feel the tempo, the kick will fall right into its proper place in each case.

With the breaststroke, however, the kick is taught at the same time as the arm stroke to learn the necessary coordination. Even though the feel will come with the balance, the balance does not seem to come as naturally here as in the other strokes. Basically this is because the arm stroke recovery occurs in the water and this throws off the whole balance of the body. Therefore you must learn the kick immediately instead of allowing your legs to laze about. Let me explain the arm stroke and you will see why.

The breastroke starts in this manner: The arms are parallel, extended straight above the head, in the same plane as the body. The legs are fully extended behind. In the breaststroke, the arms move symmetrically, pulling at the same time.

To begin the stroke you are lying in the water with relaxed arms extended forward of the head in their natural curvature. The head is down but not against the chest. The head must be continually in a relaxed state and looking forward in the breaststroke, so you don't really want to assume the extreme position of keeping the chin against the chest.

But remember, if the head is lifted too much it throws the torso deeper into the water, which is not a desirable position.

The arms in the breaststroke will pull in a similar fashion as they pull in the crawl: The palm of the hand and the forearm remain in the same plane pulling from the top of the arm stretched out forward over the head, then down and back toward the waist. Up to this point, the arms are in a very similar position to the crawl, but they are acting simultaneously.

When the arms are perpendicular to the body, stop following the crawl pattern. As you will remember, in the crawl at that point you had to bend the palm of the hand in an angle that was more acute to the forearm. However, in the breaststroke, you do not continue pushing back. This is the furthest backward extent of the stroke and here you begin the recovery portion.

When the arms are perpendicular to the body, take the palms of the hands and the forearms and, keeping them in a straight line, rotate the hand in such a manner that it appears as if you are going to clap them together at the imaginary center line on your body.

Your thumbs are now pointing out and your elbows point into your chest. As the elbows approach the chest, they will bend more and the hands begin to extend forward. At this point, the hands are going into the recovery stroke. The palms of your hands should now be in the direct line of your vision as you are looking down at the bottom of the pool. Your face is still out of the water. The palms extend forward, bringing the elbows straight out, until the arms are in the position they were in at the beginning of the stroke.

The breaststroke has approximately half the amount of pulling power as the crawl. If you remember in the crawl, you have that extra distance from the point at which the arms are perpendicular with the body (where the breaststroke begins recovery) to where the thumbs touch the tape mark on the thigh. That extra distance provides extra power.

When I say the palms are turned so that you can see them during the recovery, I am overemphasizing so that the beginner can see an obvious change in the pitch of the palms.

At the start of the recovery, when the thumbs are rotated out bringing the palms together in that clapping position, it is not essential that the palms be further turned so that they are facing up toward the face. When the arms come through and the elbows drive into the chest, it is most comfortable for me to keep the palms of my hands in the clapping position. I'm then looking at my thumbs, instead of looking into the palms of my hands.

Of course, now that your hands are extended in front of your head once more at the beginning of a new stroke, you should rotate your hands so that the palms are facing down again. The palms of the hands are in the same plane as the forearms, ready to grab new water.

The pattern that the hands follow should be studied, for the imaginary line down the center of the body is not followed exactly. As the arms begin the stroke, they go out away from the body a bit instead of pulling straight down. Then as the stroke progresses, they go back in toward the body and out again, creating an inverted "C" pattern.

The breathing in the breaststroke is very natural since the head must always remain above the water. The most natural place to fit the breathing into the breaststroke pattern is when you have the most power to compensate for that extra lift of the head. As mentioned before, in the breaststroke, the head lifts forward. You cannot breathe to the side. It is permitted, but the nature of the stroke is such that the back and shoulders should remain as level and as flat against the water surface as possible. Turning the head to the side to breathe would alter this level plane.

Speaking of this level surface, I want to mention one problem that beginning swimmers often have with the breaststroke. When you learn how to swim the stroke fairly well, you will probably have the tendency to lift your chest out of the water. This causes a bobbing effect. As the chest comes up the lower part of your torso goes down, causing more of a drag. In overcoming this drag, you will pull harder, causing the chest to rise and the torso to fall again. So you go up and down, up and down in the water.

Because of this bobbing effect it might seem to you that you are really getting a lot of power out of the breaststroke, but much of the energy and effort is expended by overcoming the drag. Besides, the bobbing effect forces the water to strike against the chest in such a manner as to cause more friction and produce even more drag. On the other hand, if the body remains flat in the water, you get the least amount of resistance, and consequently the most power and thrust.

The breath comes at the beginning of the arm stroke. When the arms are starting to pull down, the head is lifted and the chin and eyes face forward. Then when your arms are in a position perpendicular to your torso, you take a breath.

After you have inhaled, submerge your head again. At this point, the arms that were perpendicular to your chest begin to rotate to the clapping position, your elbows come into your chest, your arms extend forward, and you start the recovery.

You should also begin to exhale at this time—just as your hands pass in front of your eyes. You exhale under the water that covers your mouth.

You may take a breath every stroke or you can take a stroke without a breath by simply keeping the head and the chin down. In the breaststroke, however, it is customary to take a breath with every stroke.

Frogs were the originators of the breaststroke. When they swim their forearms stroke in the fashion just described, and they use the frog kick, naturally enough. One of the oldest swimming styles and the first competitive stroke was created by building on the stroke of the frog.

The breaststroke kick is a symmetrical one with both legs moving simultaneously, just as the arms are. When the arms are extended forward at the beginning of the stroke, the legs will be extended backward with both feet pointed. Your body is stretched out as far as possible.

In the crawl, backstroke, and butterfly kicks the ankle must remain relaxed and flexible. This is not true in the breaststroke kick.

In the beginning of the kick, the legs are extended fully and the ankles are relaxed. Then the legs are drawn forward and the knees are brought up as if you were preparing for a squatting position. Keep the knees together as they are drawn toward the chest. As the thighs become perpendicular to the torso, the ankles, which have remained loose up to this point, should be perpendicular to the calf. Now both legs thrust backwards, flipping the water in a whipping action. As the legs reach the extent of their thrust, the ankles whip the toes up and point them backward once more.

The coordination of the kick with the arm stroke will ordinarily fall into place. It is really very simple. When the arms start to pull the water and your head is lifted for your breath you begin to draw your legs toward your chest. When your arms are perpendicular to your torso, your legs should also be perpendicular. As you begin to roll your thumbs forward, put your head back down from taking your breath, and start to extend the arms forward once again, the legs begin the backward thrust.

It is precisely at the point when the arms are beginning the recovery stroke that there is a lapse in the thrust power, so it is important at this time that the legs make up for this lack by implementing their whipping action. Just as your legs reach the backward extension, creating the whip by pointing the toes, your arms should be fully extended to begin another stroke.

To recap briefly: The arms and legs should be fully extended; as the arms begin their pull, the legs come up so that the thighs are perpendicular to the chest. At that point, the hands rotate so the palms are up and the recovery stroke is begun. The legs kick backward and the whip comes at the end of the thrust as the toes are quickly pointed. The ankles are then relaxed, the arms begin their pull again and the legs are drawn forward toward the chest.

The most important aspect of the breaststroke is to coordinate the kick and the arm pull, and to remember always that the body should be as parallel to the water surface as possible. You do not want to dip your hips or to roll and pitch. In theory, your shoulders should remain in the same horizontal plane as the water surface.

The breaststroke is one in which you relax your legs when your arms are pulling and relax your arms when your legs are kicking. Each thrust has to compensate for the drag that occurs in the recovery stroke of the other.

Always remember to take your breath with your head raised as little as possible and to lower it afterwards. You do not want to rest your chin on your chest, because it must be relaxed and looking forward at all times in the breaststroke. Even so, in learning, it seems the most beneficial to exaggerate the position of the chin in relationship to the chest, and to keep the chin as low as possible as long as the eyes are above the surface of the water.

Once you have gained proficiency in the breaststroke, your head and eyes will be kept in the same plane as the back. The reason I stress that the chin be kept lower while learning, is because the beginner always seems to have a tendency to raise the head too high, to see where he is going. So I emphasize in learning all strokes to keep the chin as close to the chest as possible.

The breaststroke is the most difficult to understand without actually seeing it performed. The pictures in this chapter should be studied so that the beginner can see the position of the legs as they go through the kicking stroke—both thrust and recovery. The breaststroke is a relaxing stroke when employed in recreational swimming. But it is a difficult one when performed in competition since it employs a great amount of skill in terms of coordination.

The breaststroke starts with the arms and legs fully extended. The head is down, but not resting on the chest, and the hands are angled slightly out from the body.

The arms pull back simultaneously in a manner resembling the stroke used in the crawl. At this point you should begin to forcibly exhale.

When the arms are perpendicular to the body, they have reached the farthest backward extent of the stroke and begin recovery. The legs have remained inactive up to this point since in the breaststroke the arm thrust must compensate for the drag created by the legs and vice versa.

The hands are rotated into a clapping position and begin to extend forward until you can look into your palms. The legs are drawn up toward the squatting position.

With practice, the coordination of the kick and the arm stroke will come naturally. The arms near completion of the recovery portion of the stroke as the thighs become perpendicular to the torso, and the ankles, which were loose to this point, are bent perpendicular to the calves.

It is precisely at the point when the arms are in the recovery stroke that there is a lapse of thrust power. It is important that the kick make up for this. The legs thrust backwards, flipping the water in a whipping action as the toes are pointed.

Just as your legs reach the backward extension, creating the whip
by pointing the toes, your arms
should be fully extended to begin
another stroke.

7 | The Butterfly

THE BUTTERFLY IS a variation of the breaststroke and was officially recognized by the governing body of international swimming (FINA) in 1952. Since the butterfly is derived from the breaststroke, it can be taught using the frog kick first, adding the dolphin kick later once the arm stroke is mastered. However, I feel that the butterfly should be treated as an entirely separate stroke with an entirely separate kick. This will avoid mix-ups later on in trying to execute the kick properly.

The butterfly is a very fast and powerful stroke. Due to its jerky pulling action, however, it will probably never be performed as fast as the smoother-actioned crawl.

My world records were in the butterfly and the freestyle (or crawl) strokes, and I did better in those than I did in the breaststroke and backstroke. At least, I concentrated harder on them. In order of preference my favorite strokes are equally the butterfly and the crawl, then the backstroke, with the breaststroke coming in last.

I feel that the butterfly is the most difficult of the strokes to learn. By learning this stroke last you will be taking advantage of your confidence and ability in the water developed in learning the other strokes.

Like the breaststroke, the butterfly is a symmetrical stroke, in both the arm and the kicking actions.

To begin the butterfly, the swimmer lies facedown in the water with his chin against his chest and both arms extended above the head, palms down. The legs are extended backward with the feet approximately a foot apart.

The arms are ready to begin the recovery portion of the stroke at this point.

You can easily see from this photograph where the butterfly stroke got its name. Note the relaxed position of the wrists.

The recovery is made easier by the dropping of the head, for this enables the arms to come up out of the water and be extended forward.

The hands enter the water at an angle, thumbs first.

The arm pull in the butterfly is essentially the same as the arm pull in the crawl, with the exception that both arms pull simultaneously. When the arms are extended forward over the head and as they enter the water, they are relaxed and in their natural curvature. Do not try to keep the arms in a rigid, straight line. As you pull back keep the palms straight until they are perpendicular to the body. At that point, bend the palms forward to avoid pushing the water upward and forcing the body down into the water.

In the last foot of the underwater stroke, the palms begin to turn out with the thumbs pointing down until the arms are ready for the recovery.

In actual performance, the hand pull pattern of the butterfly will resemble two "S" curves rather than straight, or slightly curved lines. Always remember during the pull to keep the wrists straight and not let them bend or slip the water.

The breathing is very similar to the breathing in the breaststroke. When the arms enter the water to begin the pull, the head lifts. The chin points forward and the neck bends so that the head is thrown back. Here is the point at which you take a breath. While breathing the arms will have gone from the entry point in the water to a position almost perpendicular to the body.

Then the head falls back into the water, the chin returning to the chest, and the arms come out of the water to begin the recovery stroke. The recovery is made easier by dropping the head, enabling the arms to come out of the water and extend forward.

The kick must be integrated very neatly into the arm stroke pattern since it is essential to the total thrust of the butterfly. The dolphin kick is used with the butterfly. In order to visualize it, think of a dolphin maneuvering its tail back and forth from its middle. To emulate this smooth, easy motion, your ankles must be completely relaxed and you have to bend at the waist and at the knees. The undulation of the lower half of the body should come naturally to fit in with the rhythm of the arm stroke.

Either a one-beat kick or a two-beat kick can be employed in the butterfly. It is advisable for you to start with a one-beat kick and eventually work up to a two-beat, for the two-beat kick takes a great deal of energy.

The one-beat kick will enable you to maintain your balance more easily in the water. Later, when you wish to learn the two-beat kick, the second kick comes with the recovery of the arm stroke, helping you to lunge forward farther and to recover your arms in a cleaner, faster fashion.

The timing of the one-beat kick is relatively simple. As you begin the forward pull with the arms and lift your head for a breath, your legs kick down.

Then after you have taken your breath and your arms are ready to leave the water for your recovery stroke, your legs kick back up with the ankles relaxed.

While you will actually be getting thrust with both the upward and downward movements, most of the thrust derives from the downward motion, since the ankles are always relaxed.

To execute a two-beat kick, kick down when you lift your head out of the water to breathe and your arms have begun their pull. As you put your head back into the water, the legs come up again. As you begin the arm recovery, kick down again. By the time your legs have kicked up again, your arms have extended forward to enter the water and begin the pulling stroke. The legs are ready to begin the downward kick and the whole process starts over.

A definite up and down, or bobbing, effect, occurs in the butterfly. This is due to a combination of the powerful pulling action of the arms lifting the body in the water, the recovery action of the arms out of the water forcing the head and shoulders down, and the propulsive effect of the dolphin kick forcing the hips up. However, an excessive bobbing action should be avoided, for the extra up and down motion causes more drag and retards forward progress. An experienced swimmer will find that he can modulate the up and down motion to such an extent that it will be sufficient to facilitate easy breathing while not forfeiting an overall horizontal, streamlined position.

The basic movements of the butterfly are as follows: The swimmer lies facedown in the water with both arms extended above the head and palms down. His legs are extended to the rear with his feet about a foot apart. The arms enter the water to begin the pull with the hands relaxed, wrists stiff. The head lifts with the chin pointed forward ready to take a breath, at the same time the legs kick down.

The arms follow the "S" pattern as they pull through the water, changing the pitch from time to time to release the cavitation building up behind the palms. By the time the arms are perpendicular to the torso, the face is back in the water. When the arms are

As the head falls back into the water after having taken a breath, the legs will come up again as the arms are about to enter the water for another stroke.

Although there is an up-and-down, bobbing movement in the butterfly, the body should retain the horizontal, streamlined position as much as possible. Here, the full extension of the arms can be seen as they begin the stroke, following an "S" pattern.

The hands are now at the widest part of the first curve in the "S" pattern. Remember to keep the wrists straight and not let them slip water.

At the midpoint of the "S" pattern now, the pattern will be complete as the hands move outward around the body and up into the air. The hands should change their pitch from time to time to release the cavitation that will build up behind the palms.

When the arms come up out of the water, the head lifts, the chin points forward, and the neck bends so that the head is thrown back.

Then the head goes back down into the water and the chin returns to the chest; the arms are into the recovery stroke.

Note the position of the palms as they are about to slice into the water, with the thumbs down on fully extended arms.

At the beginning of the butterfly stroke, the body is lying facedown in the water with both arms extended above the head, palms down.

A definite bobbing effect occurs. The recovery action of the arms forces the head down and the kick down forces the hips up.

Keep in mind when you are pulling back with both arms that the palms are kept straight until they are perpendicular to the body. The legs, too, are kept straight in their upward thrust.

At this point in the arm stroke, the palms are bent forward to keep from pushing water upward and forcing the body down in the water. The upper portion of the body is forced upward out of the water in order to take a breath as the legs begin their downward thrust.

The kick used with the butterfly is called the dolphin kick. You must bend at the waist and at the knees just slightly. The arms and head are completely out of the water at this point.

Because the ankles are always relaxed, the most forceful thrust is obtained with the downward stroke. Here the starting position is reached and the cycle is about to begin again.

ready to begin recovering, the feet have reached their lowest point in the water and they kick back up.

As we mentioned earlier, the butterfly is the most complicated of the four swimming strokes and requires the most energy and good coordinated movements to perform. When it is performed well, it is among the most beautiful athletic events to watch.

8 | Teaching Children How to Swim

As soon as a child can understand instructions he is ready to learn how to swim. The best age varies from child to child, but three or four years is probably a good time to start lessons.

I find it is often better to teach a child with a group of perhaps three or four other children rather than teaching him alone. The method you choose, whether group or single lessons, will depend on the age and personality of the child involved. One reason it is usually easier to teach several children at the same time is that there is often a daredevil in the group, or at least one child who does something that the others are then apt to follow. And even if the demonstrator is less than perfect, he or she can build the confidence in the others to try. In each child's interpretation the feat is different, for children are fantastically individual in their imitations.

The two most important points to remember when teaching children how to swim are to build up their confidence in you as the instructor and to encourage them to relax in the water as soon as they can.

One way to build up confidence is to assure your students that the water is safe as long as you are around to help them when and if they get into difficulty. Be physically near each child as he learns a new skill and hold him up when needed. It also helps to have the pool at a comfortable 80 degrees to make it seem more like bath water—a familiar element. It would be unfortunate for children to begin learning how to swim and immediately associate the pool with feeling cold and uncomfortable.

Your first aim should be to teach the children how to swim underwater, working up to this as described in the first chapter. Start by holding one child at a time in the pool, letting him get used to the water gradually, then lowering him into the water until he can touch bottom and the water is no more than chest high on him. Let each child get used to the feeling of buoyancy, encouraging him to move his hands and feet in the water. Perhaps having the children sit in the pool where it is very shallow would be a good way to acquaint them with the floating sensation. If their legs are extended in front of them, the legs will rise off the bottom of the pool. Be sure to demonstrate each step and supervise closely.

Next, have the group hold their breath for a few seconds with their eyes closed and their faces out of the water. Then have them repeat the process in waist-deep water, putting their faces in the water. You can hold each child's hand in turn as he tries this, or have older pupils hold onto the side of the pool. Then ask them to open their eyes under the water. By steps, lead the children to submerge their entire heads.

If by chance they are too afraid and will not submerge their heads or open their eyes underwater, make a game of it. You could throw coins into the water and tell them that if they pick them up they can have them. First demonstrate for them how this is done. Tell them they must hold their breath and open their eyes as they bend over. You have to come down to their level before you can lead them up to yours.

After they have become accustomed to being underwater for a few seconds at a time and are comfortable there, teach the children some method of propulsion underwater. Have them walk on the bottom while they wave their arms about, in a semicrouch position with their heads submerged. Let them enjoy the feel of the slow-motion movement. Then begin to teach a basic stroke such as the dog paddle. There is no set method of just how to move underwater, so there is no one way to teach underwater propulsion. Of course, as your students grow more proficient in swimming, they will most likely choose some form of the breaststroke for maneuvering while underwater as that is the most efficient stroke to use.

Once they learn to propel themselves underwater and they feel comfortable, then you can begin to teach the proper techniques, but there is plenty of time for that. One thing you must not do is rush the lessons. You will probably discover that teaching children to swim underwater is easier than teaching adults, for the simple reason that many times adults have a longstanding fear of being submerged, which is hard to overcome.

After you have introduced the children to the water let them play games and just generally have fun in the water. They could play tag or compete in finding objects underwater or in counting how many fingers you are holding up in an effort to reinforce your lessons on keeping their eyes open underwater. As they are enjoying themselves they are becoming familiar with both the resistance and the buoyancy of the water. Bobbing up and down will let them get used to the water as it covers their faces even when they aren't expecting it.

The next step is to teach the back float, proceeding as already outlined in the second chapter. Take one child at a time at this point and gently support him underneath as you explain how to keep the waist stiff and the lungs half filled with air. At first the child will probably find it easier to simply hold his breath. Make

Learning to swim should be fun. After children learn to hold their breath and put their faces in the water, bobbing up and down will give them an overall feel for the pool.

Both instructor and student should enjoy the learning process and feel comfortable with one another. Here the student begins to assume the position for the back float.

In teaching the back float, the instructor should support the student's back with one hand as he explains that the arms are extended overhead, the waist is kept semistiff, and the lungs should be at least half-filled with air at all times during the float.

Success! If the child follows these simple steps he or she will soon be floating freely.

Here the children are learning the flutter kick that accompanies the crawl by holding onto the side of the pool. They need frequent reminding that their feet should not break the surface of the water.

Working with each child in turn, demonstrate to the others the techniques involved in the crawl. Here the students are being shown the full extension of the arm at the outset of the crawl.

sure the arms are extended over the head and the legs are straight, one foot apart. Also encourage the child to keep his head back in the water. Once all the children have learned how to float, have them experiment with inhaling and exhaling while floating—to experience having their bodies rise or fall depending on how much air they have in their lungs.

After the lessons on the back float have been learned, teach the children how to float on their stomachs in the prone float. Follow the same procedure, being sure to support each child with your hand on the stomach until he or she feels confident enough to per-

mit you to let go. It will be a major victory when the first student is
floating freely and the others are watching, for they will very likely
want their turns.

Don't push your pupils too hard and turn them off to swimming
altogether. Allow each child the freedom to progress at his own
pace. If a child wants more, you are going too slowly for him. But
be sure not to let him get ahead of himself. Just as with adults,
children should not proceed to the next step until they have mastered what has already been taught.

Once the floats have been mastered by the students, you can
begin teaching the crawl. The first step might be to have the children hold onto the sides of the pool and kick their feet. Follow the
instructions detailed in Chapter Four. Remind the children that
their feet should not break the surface of the water, and explain
how the leg remains straight while kicking up and bent while kicking down. Then using one child to demonstrate, explain the arm
stroke. Hold the child's arm in the correct bent-arm position and
have the others imitate. Then, while supporting the child under
the stomach, let him stroke his way across the pool while you walk
along beside. After he understands the stroke, combine the stroke
with the kick, again walking along beside the child as you support
him. The final step is to teach the correct method of breathing. In
all of this, a large dose of patience on the part of the teacher is
required. And remember to keep it light. Adapt the instructions to
take advantage of something a child does or says.

A very young child of three may not yet be physically able to
swim the crawl. A young child's center of gravity is such that he will
submerge in the water. He can still be easily taught to swim. Supporting him under the stomach, show him how to perform the dog
paddle by grabbing water alternately with one hand and then the
other and pulling each hand toward his chest in a scooping effect.
Then simply describe how to do the flutter kick and walk alongside
the child as he puts these skills into practice. Once he can do them
accurately, then show him how to breathe. While swimming on his
own he will probably submerge just below the surface of the water
if he puts his head down. Having already learned to be comfortable underwater, this should cause no problem. At frequent intervals the child will simply raise his head and take a breath, then
lower it again and continue swimming.

Support the child under his stomach and walk along with him as he practices the crawl stroke.

Proper breathing should be included in the lessons as early as possible. This pupil shows he understands the basic principles involved.

The face should turn into the water as the right hand again begins its stroke.

Once the children understand the basic mechanics of the crawl, their technique can be refined. Here the student is being shown how to bend her elbow during recovery.

The arm enters the water more cleanly when it is angled. The wrist should be kept stiff, but the hand itself relatively relaxed.

Teaching a very young child to swim is a little different procedure. The best method is to teach him to use the dog paddle underwater.

Up for air. While the child is inhaling, he continues executing the dog paddle as a form of treading water.

When first learning the backstroke, have the student practice the arm action while standing in the water.

After your pupils have mastered the crawl they can proceed to the backstroke. Again use one child as the demonstrator. Standing in waist-deep water, illustrate the backward motion of the arm stroke. Have everyone practice this while standing up. Then have your demonstrator float on his back in the water and perform the stroke he just learned while you walk along next to him with your hand under his back. The next step is to add the flutter kick. When the child is moving fairly well you can remove your hand and he should be able to continue on his own.

When your pupils have mastered these strokes you can have them practice by racing against one another or playing water games. At all times swimming should be fun for them.

At this point it might be a good idea for you to introduce the children to simple dives from the side of the pool. As explained in Chapter One, they can start with the feet-first dive, which simply involves walking off the side of the pool into the water. Proceed then to the kneeling dive, first showing them yourself how to do it. One foot rests on the edge of the pool with the toes over the edge, while the other leg is bent and the child rests on that knee. He should then extend his arms straight over the head and join his hands, leaning over the water with the head tucked in between the arms. The arms should cover the ears. Then taking a breath, he should lead with the arms and head and fall over into the water.

The basic standing dive is very similar. The child stands with his feet about six inches apart and his toes curled over the edge of the pool. His arms extend over his head, touching his ears, and he bends forward over the water. Again, taking a breath and leading with the arms and head, he should fall forward into the water. You may also wish to teach the surface dives discussed in Chapter Two at this time.

The lessons can become as detailed as you and your pupils wish. Just be sure not to go on to a more difficult lesson before the children fully understand what they have learned and can perform with ease. For further steps in teaching children how to swim, simply follow the directions given in previous chapters.

The biggest difference in teaching children to swim as opposed to adults is that they will need constant assurance that you are there to help them at all times. And, of course, you will be. If by any chance you fear for a child's safety, you are not the right instructor for him. Your fear will be quickly conveyed to him and it

The next step is for the child to use the stroke while floating on her back. As she does this, Mark supports her with his hand under her back and offers advice and encouragement.

Now combining the kick with the arm stroke, the student swims on her own.

It's exciting for both instructor and pupil when a new skill is mastered.

will be unlikely that he will learn to swim well. You should be confident in what you are teaching and in your students' ability to learn.

When teaching children always try to make learning fun. And remember not to push them too hard, or let them get overtired. Encourage them to rest at regular intervals. Learning should not be work for them, but a form of play.

Competition is a great way to encourage children to use their skills.

The kneeling dive begins with the student resting on the knee of one leg and the foot of the other. The arms are extended over the head, covering the ears.

To dive, the student simply leans over and pushes off with the foot of the kneeling leg. The head should remain between the arms.

Here the student is about to enter the water from the standing dive. The feet grab the edge of the pool, the knees are bent, and the arms are again extended over the head covering the ears.

Once all the students have mastered the standing dive, it might be fun to dive in a group, provided everyone is carefully supervised.

If they arch their backs properly, the students will not jackknife as they enter the water.

Mark and his class. While it is usually preferable to teach children in groups, don't take on more students than you feel certain you can handle.

9 | Safety Measures and Lifesaving Techniques

THE BEST SAFETY ADVICE I can give you concerning the water is *learn to swim well*. But that advice is not always enough, for there are certain instances in which you need to know other methods of dealing with survival in the water. For example, you might at some time experience a cramp while in the water, or you might find yourself too far from shore to swim back. In those and other cases it is best to understand some basic survival techniques.

The most important thing to remember is *keep cool*. Don't lose your head and go into a panic. This is something you should have been taught when you learned to swim. Your instructor should have constantly reminded you to relax. In this book, near the beginning, I warned you about the disastrous effects that fear has upon your concentration and coordination when you are learning how to swim. Not only was it true then but it continues to be true at any time you are in the water, even if you are considered to be an expert swimmer.

In the case of cramps, there are some very basic rules to follow, which you should know and use.

There is an old wives' tale about swimming right after eating which I should mention. As the story goes, if you swim directly after eating you will get stomach cramps. Well, it depends mostly on what kind of shape you are in, what you have eaten, and what type of swimming you wish to do. I guess it doesn't hurt anyone to adhere to the principle of not swimming for a half hour after eating, since most people aren't accustomed to swimming all that often. And after they have eaten, a lot of their energy and muscle power is being used to digest the food. Stomach muscles are used in swimming and if you happen to be out of condition, you may be putting too much demand on those muscles.

However, most cramps are not caused by entering the water too soon after eating. A cramp is usually caused by the effect of cold water on the muscles, by overexertion of a muscle, or by some other form of tension. And even though a cramp is painful, it is usually not dangerous—*unless* the swimmer loses his head and gives in to the pain and fear.

Although they can occur in almost every area of the body, cramps usually affect the calf or the foot. The muscles in these areas develop tight, hard knots that hinder smooth, coordinated movement. In most cases a cramp can be relieved by simply changing your position in the water, or by changing your swimming stroke.

If this does not help, gently massage the muscle that is cramped until it is relieved. Let us assume that the cramp is in the foot, calf, or thigh. You should bring your body into a prone float position while massaging the muscle, and then when the cramp is gone and you begin swimming again, remember to use a different stroke and a different kick.

If the cramp happens in another part of the body—the stomach, for example—you should float on your back and stretch to full length. This should relieve the cramp.

No matter where the cramp occurs and how fast it is relieved, you should attempt to reach the shore (or some other safe place out of the water such as a boat) as easily and quickly as possible. Remember always to keep cool; remain calm.

Perhaps the most difficult time to keep calm is when you are alone and the shore is much too far away to reach easily and the cramp seems to be getting worse. If you happen to be in this situation, you definitely should know how to do the survival float. This is basically just a floating position in which the face is in the water and the body is relaxed. It is useful in that it conserves energy and it can keep you afloat for a long period of time.

In order to perform this float, rest your body vertically in the water. The upper portion of your body will be bent and your arms will dangle, in a relaxed position. You will appear to someone watching as if you were a dead body in the water, but that is precisely what you are trying to avoid.

When resting in the floating and bobbing technique (the survival float), the head is underwater and the hands dangle at the sides.

In order to take a breath you must execute a scissors kick and push down against the water, lifting the head up.

You will start the process with air in your lungs, and as I said, your body vertical in the water. Place your face in the water so that only the back of your head and the upper portion of your back are showing above the surface. Remain in this position until you need a breath of air. Then push with your arms down against the water, kick with your legs, and raise your head above the surface just enough to breathe. Then repeat the process.

You can use the survival float for several purposes. Among them are (1) to save your energy and keep afloat until help arrives, (2) to rest for a time before striking out for shore once more, and (3) to relax until a cramp is relieved or until it goes away of its own accord. In any case, it is a very handy and a very simple float position to learn and use, one you would be well advised to add to your swimming skills.

Of course, I hardly need mention that it is always wise to look about you for possible objects to use as floats if you feel you are going to be in trouble. Even though the object may not in itself be large enough or buoyant enough to keep you afloat, its slight buoyancy may be enough to keep you afloat far longer than you would have without it.

Perhaps the most risky advice to give anyone is that concerning lifesaving methods. This is true because it is often the case that a swimmer untrained in lifesaving techniques who attempts a rescue becomes the second victim. The original victim, in a panicky frenzy, can pull the rescuer under the water and both will drown. In certain extreme cases someone trained in lifesaving may find it necessary to strike a frantic victim in such a way as to subdue him. However, this should be an exception, rather than a rule, and something a novice at lifesaving should never attempt.

If you should find yourself in a position where someone is in trouble, in all cases you should try to help him. But you should never jump into the water before all other methods of helping the victim are exhausted. Depending on the situation, you should extend a long pole, or an oar; throw a rope, or hang onto a stationary support while extending your hand.

If you are in a boat, especially a small boat such as a rowboat, and you are trying to pull someone aboard, bring the person to the stern of the boat and lift him in from there. This will keep the boat from capsizing. The method of lifting the victim is the same as that used in lifting someone from a pool, as illustrated in this chapter.

If you are tossing a floating object (such as a ring buoy) which has a rope attached, place your foot firmly on one end of the line before you toss the ring into the water. Hold the buoy in one hand and the coiled rope in the other (your foot is still firmly placed on one end of the rope) and throw both simultaneously. Try to throw the object beyond the victim. In that way, you can pull on the rope to bring it back within easy reach of the victim. When the victim has the object in his grasp, pull steadily using a hand-over-hand method.

If all possible methods of lifesaving from a ground position have been exhausted and you must jump into the water to help the victim, remember these basic rules. Always approach the victim from behind. And be prepared to break any hold that the victim may place on you.

It is often best if you can totally submerge and then approach the victim from the rear. In most cases, the victim is so interested in staying above the water that he will not go under to grab onto you.

Here Mark and his wife Suzy demonstrate a lifesaving carry in which one of the rescuer's arms crosses the victim's chest and the other pins one of the victim's arms behind her.

The same carry can be used without pinning the victim's arm.

The chin carry can be used on an unconscious or semiconscious victim.

Mark demonstrates one method of blocking a victim's attempt to grab the
rescuer's head. Bring your arms up quickly between the victim's arms.
In lifting a victim from a pool put both of the victim's hands on the edge
of the pool and hold onto them as you climb out.

Then grab both wrists and drop the victim down straight into the water a bit (not over the head) in order to get momentum for the lift-out.

Lift the victim straight up.

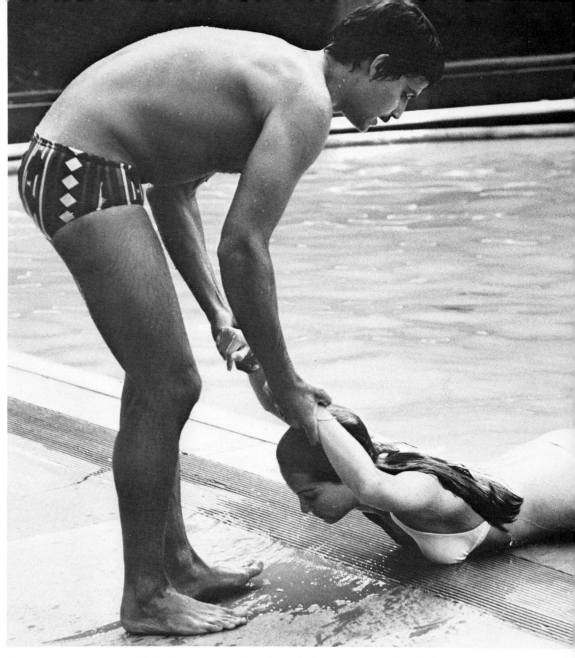

Place the upper part of the body over the edge of the pool onto the deck and then lift the legs from the water.

A carry I recommend is one that takes some strength. You should grab the victim's left arm with your left arm and pin it behind him while placing your other arm across his chest. Your right arm will pass under both the victim's arms. In this carry your legs must provide all the propulsion, using the kick from the side-stroke or the flutter kick. (A variation of this carry omits pinning one of the victim's arms behind him, which enables you to stroke with your free arm.)

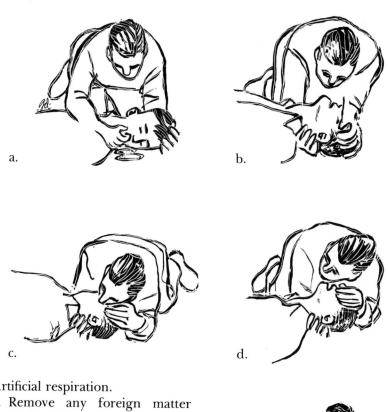

a.

b.

c.

d.

Artificial respiration.
a. Remove any foreign matter from the victim's mouth.
b. Tilt back the head.
c. Seal your mouth over the victim's and exhale.
d. Listen for exhalation.
e. One or more sharp blows between the shoulder blades may be needed to dislodge an obstruction in the breathing passages.

e.

There is also the chin tow—a method by which the victim is grasped under the chin with one of your hands as you tow him to shore. This will only work effectively with a semiconscious or unconscious victim.

If the rescue is made in a swimming pool, there is a proper way of lifting the victim onto the deck. Place both of the victim's hands on the edge and hold onto them while you climb out. Then grab both wrists and drop the victim back into the water a bit so that you can gain momentum and pull him out more easily. Lift the upper portion of the body over the edge and maintain a strong grip as you lift the legs up from the water.

The expired air method of artificial respiration, or what is more commonly called mouth-to-mouth resuscitation, is currently the most widely approved form of artificial respiration.

In performing mouth-to-mouth resuscitation, place the victim on his back and quickly make sure there is no foreign matter in his mouth. Tilt his head fully backward by placing one hand under his neck and the other hand on top of his head. When the tilt has been achieved, move the hand under the neck to the victim's chin, opening the mouth. Make sure that the tongue is forward in the mouth so that he does not choke. Pinch the nose closed. Open your mouth wide and place it tightly around the victim's mouth. Watch the victim's chest to determine when it expands and stop blowing when it does. Remove your mouth and listen for any expiration. If the chest does not rise, check again to make sure that the breathing passages are free of obstruction. You might have to turn the victim on his side and strike him sharply between the shoulder blades to dislodge whatever is obstructing the breath.

Begin the resuscitation at a rapid rate and then lessen the rate until you are administering one breath every five seconds.

If the victim is smaller, such as a child, you may wish to seal your mouth over the victim's mouth and nose. And the breaths should be shorter. Under *no* circumstances should you blow violently into a baby's lungs.

Although artificial respiration can be carried out following the instructions above, I feel strongly that it is best to have actual physical instruction given to you by a competent instructor. And I recommend that everyone who can, participate in such a safety program.

Never go swimming in places you know nothing about, especially when you are alone. And in all cases try to go swimming with a companion. I think this is one of the most important rules to follow since you cannot depend on the elements. Also, an accident might occur—you could hit your head on a rock while diving, or perhaps cut yourself in some way. Another factor to consider is that it is usually cold in lake or ocean swimming, and an inexperienced swimmer is prone to cramp in cold water. Then again, if you are caught in a strong tide, it is good to have someone there who can help you or go and get help.

On occasion you might have to swim against a current. There are some basic rules to remember when doing so. Never buck the current if you can help it. And let the current work with you, or at least hinder your progress as little as possible.

A rip current, flowing outward from the shore, can cause a lot of difficulty unless you know how to deal with it. Swim across the current at a right angle until you are free of its pull. Then turn and head for shore.

There is no way to swim around a littoral current—one which runs parallel to the shore. You must swim across it. You may be carried for a distance, but eventually you will be able to cross it and

a. Swim across a rip current at a right angle and then head for shore.

b. Swim across a littoral current toward shore.

c. Swim diagonally across a current that runs at a diagonal to the shore.

reach shore. In a current that runs diagonally to the shoreline, you must swim diagonally across it and then head for shore.

I love the ocean and it can be great fun, but it is dangerous and should be treated with respect.

10 | Racing Starts and Turns

THERE ARE ONLY two basic types of starts in competitive swimming: starts in the water and starts out of the water. Out-of-the-water starts are used in the freestyle, the breaststroke, and the butterfly. The backstroke is the only one that uses in-the-water starts.

Out-of-the-water starts can be executed in three ways. The original method of the hands-backward start is rarely used today. The standard racing start, which is most often used, is called the hands-forward start. The newest—and I think the fastest—is the grab start which was perfected in the seventies. It is the one I used and helped to perfect. I consider it the best start of the three, of course.

Whichever start you use, you should remember if you are swimming the breaststroke or the butterfly, you should push yourself off in such a manner as to dive just slightly deeper—maybe a foot or so—than if you were swimming the freestyle. This is because the breaststroke and the butterfly require a kick and a pull underwater and if you are not deep enough, you cannot utilize the water properly. In the freestyle (the crawl) you will want to enter the water properly so that you end up in a relatively flat position in relation to the surface of the water.

Let's take the original starting dive first. You will approach the block and address it by standing at the block at ease, with your feet spread approximately one foot apart. Your arms should hang loosely at your sides. The toes are placed at the forward (leading) edge of the starting block. You may curl your toes around the block or just stand there, whichever way you feel the most comfortable.

(LEFT): In the hands-backward start, first address the block with your feet and face forward, standing at ease with your arms hanging at your sides. (CENTER): When the command "Take your mark!" is given, bend slowly forward, flex your knees, and move the hands backward. (RIGHT): You must be balanced so finely that you are almost, but not quite, ready to topple into the water.

(LEFT): When the gun is sounded, throw your arms forward and push off from the block in a driving force. (CENTER): After the feet have left the block, you should spring out over the water with your back arched. (RIGHT): The head points down, the legs are straight, and the waist is semistiff. If performed properly, you will enter the water cleanly.

The commands for the start are: "Timers and judges ready!," "Take your mark!," and then the gun will be fired. In competitive swimming the timekeeper is located to the swimmers' rear while the judge is located at the side of the pool.

When the command "Take your mark!" is given, you will bend slowly forward, flexing your knees a bit to maintain your balance. As you do so your head is turned forward and slightly down, but your eyes should be fixed on the far end of the pool.

Your hands, which were at the side, slowly come back so that they are positioned in the same plane as the back, which is now bent forward. At this point you have to maintain a delicate balance while leaning forward so that you can roll on the balls of your feet. You must be just on that fine edge where you are almost, but not quite, out of balance.

When the gun is sounded, you must be ready to quickly throw your arms forward and push off from the block in a driving force. The arms are now fully extended above the head, but there is no need to clasp the hands together or even place them near one another. Rather they should be stretched forward in a position similar to that used for starting the butterfly or breaststroke while lying in the water.

The head is down and the body is now fully extended. The feet have left the block, the head faces down and the legs are straight. Your waist should be in that stiff but semirelaxed state that was taught for the floating and backstroke position.

The hands enter the water first with the head, torso, and finally legs and feet following. One serious fault a swimmer might easily have in his starting dives is jackknifing. When this happens the feet hit the water first and the arms next, or the hands and feet hit at the same time. This occurs when the waist is allowed to bend and the legs come down.

Once you have entered the water, your back should arch a bit, so that you will come quickly back up to the surface. Then with both arms extended, begin the strokes.

A good way to think about the starting dive, as you try it, is to try to feel as if your body is a spear that has been thrown into the water in a slight arc. Your body should follow that same smooth arc in entering the water.

In the butterfly, as I mentioned, you should dive just a bit deeper than if you were going to swim the crawl stroke. Then when you hit the water, you will arch the back just a bit, so that you come quickly back to the surface with both hands extended. You begin the stroke, lifting your head for your first breath.

The same applies for the breaststroke. Dive in about a foot deeper than for the crawl, arch your back, and take your first stroke. At the inception of the stroke, your legs should rise for the kick. You will then break the surface, lift your head for a breath, and continue your stroking.

In the second type of out-of-the-water start, which is really the standard racing start, the swimmer again addresses the swimming block in the same manner.

When the starter says "Take your mark!," bend your knees in the same manner as previously explained. However, instead of having your hands swing to the rear, your hands will come forward and dangle completely relaxed, as if you were going to bend down and touch your toes. Keep your hands approximately five or six inches away from your toes by flexing your knees. Now, with your knees bent in that fashion, when the gun sounds, bring your arms up and out at the sides as if you were just swinging them outward. The natural tendency, as your feet push off from the block and the body thrusts forward, is to bring the arms down again toward your rump and then up and out in front. The movement is similar to a butterfly stroke—but just the opposite. The arm swing itself helps create momentum for the drive forward.

The standard racing start is the one I used before I began using the grab start. I never used the hands-backward start. When I was swimming in the sixties, the standard racing start was the one most coaches and swimmers used.

However, the start I really used the most and think is the best is the grab start. It helps you to assume that really fine balance that is needed for a good start; with this dive you are poised right on the edge of the block, up on your toes.

Of course, you don't want to be standing flat-footed in any starting dive; that is obvious. You want to be on your toes. Otherwise it takes too much time to come forward, to lean enough to get yourself off the block.

In the grab start, you again address the block in the same manner and stand relaxed with your arms hanging at your sides. At the command "Take your mark!," spread your feet apart just a bit more so that they are about fourteen or fifteen inches apart. Bend

(LEFT): In the standard or hands-forward racing start, you again address the swimming block in the same manner. When the command "Take your mark!" is given, your hands should dangle in front of you and your knees should be flexed. (RIGHT): When the gun sounds, you will begin to bring the arms up and out to the sides of the body.

144

The movement of the arms is similar to that of a butterfly stroke, only reversed.

(LEFT) The natural tendency, as your feet push off and the body goes forward is to bring the arms down again toward the rump and forward. (RIGHT) The arm swing itself helps create momentum for the drive forward as the feet leave the block. The back arches slightly, the head is down, and the hands are extended ready to enter the water.

over, with your arms dangling down at the front, grab the starting block under the lip. This way, if you start to roll forward, you can hold yourself by rolling back on the balls of your feet and pulling your arms into the block, thereby holding yourself in that fine balance. I keep my arms bent a little in the natural curvature—but slightly tensed so that I can readily control my balance.

In the grab start, your knees will be bent a little bit more than in the two previous starts in order to reach down to the lip of the starting block.

When the gun goes off, your arms swing straight out and you squat even lower for the push-off. The arms are extended above your head and you enter the water the same way you did on the other dives.

This dive does require a bit more skill and I suggest you don't use it until you have mastered the standard racing start. The main difficulty in accomplishing this dive successfully is that you are lower in relation to the surface of the water, so when you push off, it is essential that you leap up in this dive instead of simply leaping forward. Your body must go up into a more pronounced arc in order to enter the water cleanly. Because of this more pronounced arc, it is more difficult for the amateur swimmer to avoid jackknifing in the water. The leap up has a tendency to drag the feet down and so what you have to do when you leap up is to throw the back of your feet up at the same time. After your body comes up into that arc, it will descend in the form of a smooth, natural dive. If performed properly, the diver will enter the water cleanly, and a good distance out from the block.

When you start from the standard racing position, you might be able to hit the water at three or four feet beyond the block with relatively little trouble. That is not true of the grab-start method. You are closer to the water surface, as we mentioned, and therefore you tend to hit the water sooner. You will get off the block faster, but you'll hit the water sooner and therefore you will lose all the advantage you have gained. So, in order to compensate for this tendency to hit the water sooner, you must jump higher with a great deal of force and try to hit the water some three or four feet out from the edge as you would have using the standard racing dive. The advantage is, of course, that you have reached that distance away from the edge of the pool sooner than you would have using the old

(LEFT): A head-on look at the grab start. With this dive you must be poised right on the edge of the block, up on your toes. (RIGHT): As the gun goes off, the arms swing straight out and you should squat even lower for the push-off.

(LEFT): The main difficulty in accomplishing this dive successfully is that you are lower in relation to the surface of the pool. It is essential that you leap up a little instead of simply leaping forward. (RIGHT): Only practice will enable you to enter the water without jackknifing.

A side view of the grab start. You can see that the knees are bent a bit more than in the two previous starts.

As the gun goes off, the arms swing straight up and out and the body squats even lower for the push-off.

When the dive is performed properly, the body comes up in a smooth, natural arc and the hands enter the water first.

method. You are entering the water at a faster speed, also, and that momentum will help carry you forward.

In 1971, the grab start was just being initiated and all the rules allowed its use. But if there was no lip on the starting block to grab, this was impossible. Some blocks were made with a great distance between the top and the first indentation. In order to grab the block, the swimmer would have to reach a far greater distance than was comfortable or practical—as much as a foot more. At the AAU competition in 1971, this was the case. I talked to the carpenter the night before the meet was to begin and I asked him to cut just one block a little higher so I could reach down and grab it. It took me two or three hours to convince him to do just one while he was working on the blocks. I finally persuaded him. But after he'd cut one higher he had to do them all so that one swimmer wouldn't have an unfair advantage.

The backstroke is the only in-the-water start. Every starting block usually has a little bar located at the back of the block onto which the swimmer can grab. If not, the leading edge of the block can be used. The hold is located approximately eighteen inches to two feet

Here the back is beginning to arch. The body should enter the water head first, in a relatively flat plane.

But if you ever do the dive this way, you'll remember what you did wrong and correct it the next time, because it really hurts.

Now that you have learned the starting dives the next step is to learn how to turn around once you have reached the other end of the pool.

Of the four strokes, two of them require that the swimmer hit the wall at exactly the same time with both hands. Those, of course, are the symmetrical strokes—the breaststroke and the butterfly. The freestyle and the backstroke do not even require the swimmer to touch the wall. There are two types of turns, therefore, the touch turn and the no-touch turn.

The touch turn for the crawl is performed in the following manner. As you near the end of the pool you touch with one arm. At that moment, turn the plane of your shoulder sideways and tuck your legs up forward, toward your chest, letting your momentum carry you forward as close to the wall as you can. Let go of the wall when your body starts pulling away. Your legs, which are tucked into your chest, will enable you to roll over. If you touch with your right hand, you will tuck your legs up and then when you roll over to your left side, you will let go of the wall and bring your hand immediately up to assume a stretched-out position with both arms above your head. At the same time, push off the wall, driving forward. You'll find yourself starting away from the wall on your side, and then slowly rolling over to your stomach and beginning the crawl stroke again.

In the backstroke, come to the wall and hit with your hand—say your right hand. As you touch the wall, roll your body over to your right shoulder and to a position similar to that which you used in the crawl. Tuck your knees forward and draw your body up to the wall, but instead of rolling over on your left side, stay on your back. Then let go of the wall and thrust your hands forward in a similar posture to that in starting the backstroke. Push off the wall with your feet, stretch out, and then begin the arm stroke with the left arm.

In the breaststroke, you will approach the wall with both hands. Pull your body up to the wall with your arms and tuck your legs into your chest, turning over onto your left side. Drive your arms forward and push off the wall with your feet. At that time roll your body over so that your stomach is flat, or at least parallel to the bottom of the pool. Then push off and start a stroke. Push out a little

In the backstroke, come to the wall and hit with your right hand in preparation for the touch turn.

As you touch, begin to roll the body over to the right shoulder, bringing the legs up.

The knees are brought forward and the body is drawn up to the wall while you remain on your back.

Push off the wall with the feet, stretching out and initiating the arm strokes once again.

The left hand should reach back in the backstroke grabbing water as the feet complete the push from the wall. This turn is executed in the same manner for the crawl.

In making the turn for the butterfly and the breaststroke, both hands must touch the wall at the same time.

The body is pulled up to the wall and the legs are tucked into the chest.

As the legs come up into the chest, turn onto the left side.

Drive the arms forward, push off the wall with your feet, and roll over.

Finish the push-off with the body parallel to the bottom of the pool, ready to stroke.

deeper in the breaststroke, so that your body will remain completely in the water.

The butterfly turn is performed in a similar fashion. When the arms come to the edge of the pool and the hands touch, bring the body up to the wall—exactly as if you were doing a breaststroke—and tuck your legs into your chest, rolling over onto your left side and then pushing off the wall with your feet. Roll back to your stomach and begin stroking. Again you should remember to push off a bit deeper so that the body remains completely in the water.

All of the foregoing turns are touch turns, and should be mastered first. The no-touch turn is usually performed in association with the flip turn, because that is practically the only way to do it. You cannot use the no-touch turn with the butterfly or the breaststroke, for as we said before, the rules do not permit it. It would be too difficult to use it in those events in any case. The no-touch turn is officially allowed only in the freestyle events.

The flip turn can be used with the backstroke or with the crawl, and can be performed with or without touching the wall. In the

In executing the no-touch flip turn in the crawl, you do not have to touch the wall with your hands.

When the left arm is approximately one stroke from the wall, begin to duck your head.

Do a complete somersault so that your feet go back to touch the wall.

When the flip is almost completed the arms reach forward over the head
as the feet approach the wall.

Begin to roll back over onto your stomach and extend the arms in preparation for a new stroke.

Then push off the wall as the hands come together over your head and you continue to roll onto the stomach.

From this fully extended position, roll a bit more onto your stomach and begin stroking again.

flip using the touch, the moment your hand touches the wall, drop your head underneath the water and execute a complete somersault. You'll find that when the somersault is performed, the legs will come up and flip against the wall. You will be on your back and your hands will drive forward in front of your head. As you push off, roll back over on your stomach so that your head is down and then begin the crawl stroke again.

Performing the flip turn without touching the wall is accomplished as follows: When your arm (let's say it's the left) is approximately one stroke from touching the wall (about two feet away) it should stop stroking and the right arm should make one more stroke. Duck your head and do a complete somersault. Your legs should come up to meet the wall at this point. Your hands are at your sides and as you throw your head back, thrust your arms back over your head and push off the wall, rolling onto your stomach, and begin the crawl stroke once more.

The flip turn with the touch can be used in the backstroke. As you near the wall, touch with your right arm as if you were touching the wall in a regular turn. But this time when you touch let the momentum carry you for an extra second and the right arm collapse slightly so that your head starts to move into the wall. Then the right arm, touching the wall, should push up enabling you to drop your head back and tuck your legs forward. Your body will flip over completely so that you are facing down. After your legs meet the wall, push off.

You will have to get onto your back again, so when you are pushing off the wall, roll your body back over to your side to correct the position. The natural way to do this is to take a stroke with the arm that touched the wall, forcing the body over onto your back once more. Take the stroke off to the side and when completed you will be in a perfect position to take your first left-hand regular stroke.

11 | Competitive Swimming

THE FOUR SWIMMING STROKES we've discussed (not counting the sidestroke and elementary backstroke) are all performed in individual competitive events using 50-meter pools. The world records that are recognized for individual competitive swimming are: the 100-, 200-, 400-, 800-, and 1,500-meter freestyle; the 100- and 200-meter backstroke; the 100- and 200-meter breaststroke; and the 100- and 200-meter butterfly.

Two other events in which records are recognized for individuals are the 200- and 400-meter individual medleys. The individual medley is a combination of all four of the previous swimming strokes. In swimming the event, the butterfly stroke must be performed first, then the backstroke, the breaststroke, and finally the crawl or freestyle.

The individual medley is for those talented swimmers who can swim all four strokes very well. Sometimes individual medley world record holders have a tendency to be extremely fast butterfly swimmers, or fast backstroke, breaststroke, or crawl swimmers. It does not necessarily show that the winner is outstanding in all of the strokes, for he might excel in only one. It is also true that he could just be a better swimmer in the individual medley because he delights in swimming all the strokes and can put them all together for a winning effort.

There are also three different relays that are recognized as world record events: The first is the sprint relay with a team consisting of four swimmers, each of whom swims the freestyle 100 meters for a team total of 400 meters. The distance relay in which each of the four members swims 200 meters is the second. Two hundred meters is not really much of a distance, but the relay is so called anyway. The freestyle stroke is used and the world record is recorded under the official title of the 800-meter freestyle relay.

The third relay is called the 400-meter medley relay. Four participants swim four different strokes during the event. The first swimmer uses the backstroke, the next the breaststroke, the third the butterfly, and the last the freestyle. Here the strokes follow a different order than they do in the individual medley relay.

In the butterfly, backstroke, and breaststroke events, the swimmer has to swim the stroke for which the event is named. In the freestyle, however, the swimmer can swim any stroke he wishes, provided the stroke he starts with is the stroke he finishes with. In other words, if you were swimming a 100-meter freestyle in a 50-meter pool, it would be a two-lap event. You can swim it all backstroke, all breaststroke, or all whatever, but you can't swim the backstroke for one lap and the breaststroke for the other. It is true that the crawl is the stroke usually chosen because it is the fastest, and that is why the crawl is now often referred to as the freestyle stroke.

The records in the freestyle event work this way. Assume that I have just swum the butterfly in the freestyle and I won the competition with a 53.1 time. I presently hold the butterfly record at 54.2. Would I get credit for having broken my own butterfly record? No. It wouldn't count because it wasn't in the butterfly event. As far as the freestyle event goes, the record is 51.2, so I didn't break any records. I simply won the race.

(If you wish to obtain the current rules for competitive swimming write to the Amateur Athletic Union of the United States, 3400 West 86th Street, Indianapolis, Indiana 46268.)

I definitely think improvements should be made in competitive swimming, especially concerning the Olympic and the AAU committees. A greater effort should be taken by the people on the organizing committees to work out a closer relationship between their rules and the ideals held by the competing athletes. After all, the athletes are the most important part of any competition.

A few words about training in swimming. Ever since I was very young, the distance events seemed easiest for me. I am happy that this was true, for having a distance background and training enabled me, as I got older and stronger, to handle myself in any event, whether distance or sprint. So in my opinion it is best to train first for distance events. This pays off, for it enables you to develop the stamina and conditioning that will sustain you in the sprints later on.

I was able to swim the mile (1,500-meter freestyle) when I was fourteen years old. Later, after I was eighteen, I could sustain myself in the sprints so that I wouldn't "die" at the last ten or fifteen meters. So I highly recommend that you train first for distance swimming and then later switch to sprints as you become strong enough to handle them.

Another recommendation I would make is don't burden yourself with too many "essentials" that you feel you *have* to do in order to swim well. If it ever gets to the point where you can't do them, you might psyche-out. For example, suppose I had planned on having steak and eggs every morning before swimming and especially on the day of a big competition. If the day of the big meet arrived and I couldn't get my steak and eggs, I would probably become upset and be unable to perform at my top level.

Try to keep your training on a basic level so there will be little or no ritual when it comes time to perform. The only ritual you should have to worry about is the actual performance.

In fact, my performance in the Olympics of 1972 was more of a production or ritual than it was a physical contest since all of the physical training was completed prior to the Olympics. I told the reporters, when they asked me how I thought I was going to perform, that I was "prepared." The training was over. It was too late to worry about whether or not I had swum enough laps or if I had followed my training procedures properly. The time had come to actually do it. When you get to the Super Bowl, it is the culmination of plans and techniques worked out throughout the course of the season. On the day of the competition, you have to wake up and get ready, but it's just a thing you do. I do feel "to each his own," but for me, and my experience throughout the years bears this out, it is best to keep my needs basic and avoid any "trauma-producing" missing essentials.

I should also mention that I never let my social life interfere with my athletic training. I set my standards early so that I would never get wrapped up in that manner.

I could tell you that Mark Spitz did this differently and that differently, but the only thing I really did was that I swam a little faster than everybody else and that's it!

Before a meet the only specific thing I did was swim in the water, what swimmers call warming up or just slowly loosening up—getting loose. I might have swum 1,000 or 2,000 meters, which wasn't a whole heck of a lot because we would be training between 10,000 and 20,000 meters in one workout every day. So I would just get in the pool and swim the 2,000 meters that would take maybe 40 minutes or so, just easy swimming. I'd do a little kicking, a little pulling, a little thrashing about. And then I'd relax by bobbing up and down just trying to stretch my legs.

There was one small ritual I did allow myself. I took time to think quietly. I used to make it a point before I went to bed to think about the meet the next day for maybe five minutes. Then I would put it out of my mind and go play cards or something else. Then I'd wake up in the morning and think about it again just before breakfast. Then a couple of minutes before I would get up for the competitive event, I would do it again. I would concentrate on what I wanted to do, how my competition was swimming, how well I felt, and then I would go in and swim.

There are a few tricks you can use during training since you have to think about something while you are swimming back and forth, back and forth. I used to think of different things to keep my interest up. For instance, once I used the image of a beautiful girl at the other end and I would really be swimming hard to get to her. It was a kind of a game. You couldn't be thinking of a girl all the time since that'd get to be old hat. But you have to think of something at least part of the time since after a while training gets to be a lot of dull, hard work.

It's a different story during competition. You really have to "psyche yourself up." Psyching yourself up has to do with knowing your competition. If you know that the guy next to you on the left is going to go out and swim a little faster than you the first half of the race, then you're not going to be shocked if he's ahead of you. Or if you know that the guy on your right side can't swim very fast, you have to be prepared when he turns out to be ahead of you at the beginning of the race. In other words, you have to know your competition at all times.

If you are "up and coming" as a swimmer you also have to be aware that the other swimmers are watching you and sizing you up.

They know how you have performed before and what your personal habits are. So while you are sizing up the competition, the competition is doing the same to you.

I always had a fast finish and if I were within a body length of someone during a competition, he might as well go home. That was my reputation. A competitor of mine might have thought to himself: "If I'm going to beat Spitz, I had better be out in front of him, because he'll catch me at the last lap." Also, if someone were ahead of me, he might get psyched up and think to himself, "Hey, man! I'm really hauling!"

As you become more and more successful as a swimmer and finally get to be number one, you become the hunted. It's always a lot easier to be the hunter than it is to be the hunted.

A lot has been written about the Mexican Olympics of 1968. Going into those Olympics, I held six world records. Three were in relays and three in individual events. All I wanted to do was to swim the events that I thought I could possibly win. I felt that I should compete in every event in which I held a world record. If I was the world record holder, I'd be the best in the race. So why not swim it?

As it turned out, I didn't do that well, although I didn't do anything very differently in the 1972 games. In my second Olympic competition, I was considered the old man trying to make a comeback, and the press actually sympathized with me. A reporter for *Time* magazine started off a cover story about me like this:

> Scene I: Mexico City, 1968. A gawky youngster of 18 who looks as if he could be Jerry Lewis' younger brother, perfunctorily addresses a putt. On the course beside him is his swimming coach and constant companion, Sherman Chavoor. Since the boy had recently boasted that he would become the first Olympian to win six gold medals, he needs all the relaxing he can get. Not today. A passerby happens to spot him on the green and shouts, "Hey, Jew boy, you aren't going to win any gold medals!" The brutal slur is delivered by one of the youth's comrades on the U.S. men's swimming team.
>
> Scene II: Munich, 1972. A sinewy young man of 22, who looks as if he could be Omar Sharif's younger brother, confidently strides through the Olympic Village. Surrounding him is a retinue of coaches and teammates—the entourage of an athletic eminence. At the village entrance, dozens of jock groupies strain to touch him, plead for his autograph. Inside, competitors from other countries seek his signature. "Oh, look!" cries a delighted U.S. mermaid, "There he is!" Journalists pursue him into the shower before prac-

tice. People persistently ask: Can he win seven gold medals? Yes, he answers with quiet confidence.

All I told the press was "Look, I'm just going to try to do my best." Well, they got tired of listening to that after I won five gold medals and then six gold medals. And they said, "Well, how do you think you're going to do?" And I said, "Well, I'm just going to try to do my best. I'm really happy with what I have now, and I'm glad I'm doing as well as I am. . . ."

But to get back to training . . . the perfect training temperature for a pool, as I mentioned earlier, is roughly 80 degrees. Any warmer takes too much energy out of you, and any colder becomes too cold and you become tense and uncomfortable. However, swimming in competition in 75-degree water won't bother you at all.

There are also differences in pools that you will eventually learn to "read" in order to adjust your performance. Some pools are "fast" pools and others are "slow." For the most part whether a pool is fast or slow is determined by its physical construction, especially in the gutter system. The drainage on a well-designed pool maintains the water at the correct level. Water is constantly added to the pool to replace the water lost as waves splash over the gutter. When a pool is not at its proper level, the waves hitting against the sides create a turbulence that will bother the swimmers and adversely affect their performance. Some slow pools have a tremendous amount of wave action.

The feeling you get just from looking at a pool and its surroundings also has a lot to do with whether or not it is fast. A pool can affect you psychologically and your swimming will reflect this. If the pool is clean and pleasing to the eye and if you feel that you are swimming in front of interested spectators your performance will be better than if these factors were missing.

The mental attitude of an athlete has a lot to do with how he performs. Swimming is physical when you are training. But after all the training is over, and you are in competition, swimming becomes mostly mental. It's too late to worry about whether or not you trained too hard or not enough—and if you do worry about such things during a competition, you can bet you won't perform at your best.

Many people ask me what exercises other than swimming a swimmer should practice. In my opinion, there is no substitute for swimming except more swimming. I followed very few weightlifting routines, although there are weight programs that can be done along with just regular loosening-up exercises. These are usually classified as dry-land exercises and should be done under the supervision of a coach. The exercises are also divided into those that are best for certain strokes. For example, the butterfly swimmer might want to do some strengthening exercises with weights to develop stronger arm and chest muscles. He would also want to do stretching exercises such as squat thrusts with push-ups and other exercises for the stretching and strengthening of the ankle muscles. If you want to take up a full program of dry-land exercises, see your coach or obtain a copy of Doc Counsilman's *The Science of Swimming,* which contains a well-detailed series of exercises for swimmers.

I really do believe that a dry-land exercise program that is routinely followed is a poor substitute for swimming. Some people require such a program because they believe that they need to build bulging muscles. Development of the wrong muscles, however, will add unnecessary weight. I still maintain that there is no substitute for swimming for building swimming muscles.

Other than the basic calisthenics and loosening-up exercises, I did not follow any exercise program. You should do basic loosening-up exercises, however, for it is not good to jump into the pool cold and start performing.

Before you jump into the water, you might do a few shaking exercises that consist of standing up and shaking the arms back and forth. Whirl the arms in a windmill action to loosen the shoulders and bend up and down touching your toes. Your knees should be flexed a few times, and in general simulated swimming strokes should be acted out. Basically, the whole effect is movement—shaking the legs back and forth, relaxing the wrists and the ankles, maybe sitting down and rubbing your muscles a bit.

Further loosening-up exercises are done in the water. Jump in and engage in some casual swimming. The specific warm-ups are dependent on the individual, but they include a little kicking, and some pulling and stroking movement.

As far as food goes, I simply followed a well-balanced diet and

Before you jump into the water, do a few loosening and shaking movements. Perhaps start by swinging the arms back and forth.

If you swing your arms as widely as you can in a plane parallel to the ground, you will loosen up your shoulders as well as your arms.

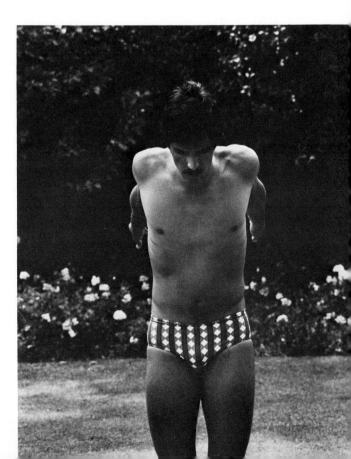

Bending over will loosen the muscles in your back and along the back of your legs.

Swing your arms over your head while still bending over to loosen the shoulders as well as the back

You can repeat these movements until you feel limber.

Any bending or stretching exercises are suitable. This one stretches the muscles in front of the leg.

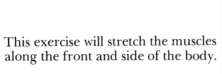

This exercise will stretch the muscles along the front and side of the body.

You might save this exercise for last. It's really an excellent tension-reliever for the back, shoulder, and neck muscles.

Feel free to improvise.

drank plenty of liquids. In any type of athletic endeavor the body needs a lot of liquid because you are constantly burning it off as energy. I do feel it is advisable to eat high protein foods, and stay away from greasy foods. Here are some foods that I feel you should avoid and some that I feel are good for you.

Avoid:

mayonnaise, gravy, potato chips, processed cheddar-type cheeses, soft drinks, imitation fruit drinks, soda, pastries, pies, cakes, candy bars.

Recommended:

2 or more servings daily of beef, veal, pork, lamb, poultry, fish, or eggs; 4 or more servings daily of a citrus fruit or any other fruit or vegetable that is a good source of vitamin C; a dark green or deep-yellow vegetable that is a good source for vitamin A—at least every other day (also other vegetables or fruits); at least two cups of milk each day, 4 servings daily of whole grain, enriched or restored.

There is one other thing I will recommend concerning food. During competition, especially, you should never put yourself on a different type of diet all of a sudden. If I were to start eating steak and eggs for breakfast when my body was not accustomed to it, I would use up valuable energy trying to digest it and my whole body would be thrown out of rhythm.

In addition to nutritional food I took the standard multiple vitamin tablets and an extra 500 mg of vitamin C. But I was not a pill freak and I do not think that anyone should be.

I have always swum immediately after eating; I used to eat breakfast and then ten minutes later I was in the water. I ate a breakfast that consisted of three or four eggs, toast, and bacon or sausage. I had a couple of glasses of milk or orange juice and then I would jump immediately into the water. But that was on a competitive level and I was used to swimming on a full stomach.

Actually swimming or any type of exercise is very healthy for you after eating—if you are in relatively good physical condition, of course—because it helps you to digest your food thoroughly and it keeps you from putting on too much weight. The worst thing you can do is to eat and then lie down for a rest.

In any case, I hope I have helped you gain a better enjoyment of the water, and perhaps even started you toward your own great swimming career.

Index